# INTRODUCTION TO SOCIALISM

Leo Huberman
Paul M. Sweezy

AAKAR

INTRODUCTION TO SOCIALISM
Leo Huberman and Paul M. Sweezy

© Monthly Review Press 1968
© Aakar Books for South Asia 2010

Published in agreement with Monthly Review Press, New York for publication and sale only in the Indian Subcontinent (India, Pakistan, Bangladesh, Nepal, Maldives, Bhutan & Sri Lanka)

All rights reserved. No part of this book may be reproduced or transmitted, in any form or by any means, without prior permission of the publisher.

First Published in India, 2010

ISBN 978-93-5002-074-6 (Pb)

*Published by*
**AAKAR BOOKS**
28 E Pocket IV, Mayur Vihar Phase I, Delhi 110 091
Phone : 011 2279 5505 Telefax : 011 2279 5641
aakarbooks@gmail.com; www.aakarbooks.com

*Printed at*
Mudrak, 30 A, Patparganj, Delhi 110 091

# CONTENTS

PREFACE . . . . . . . . . . . . . . . . . . 5

FREEDOM UNDER CAPITALISM AND SOCIALISM
    by Leo Huberman . . . . . . . . . . . . . . 7

THE ABC OF SOCIALISM
    by Leo Huberman . . . . . . . . . . . . . . 21
        I. Socialist Analysis of Capitalism . . . . . . . 23
        II. Socialist Indictment of Capitalism . . . . . . 39
        III. Advocates of Change . . . . . . . . . . 51
        IV. Socialism . . . . . . . . . . . . . . . 60

MARXIAN SOCIALISM
    by Paul M. Sweezy . . . . . . . . . . . . . 83

THE RESPONSIBILITY OF THE SOCIALIST
    by Leo Huberman . . . . . . . . . . . . . . 95

AN ECONOMIC PROGRAM FOR AMERICA
    by Paul M. Sweezy . . . . . . . . . . . . . 103

LESSONS OF SOVIET EXPERIENCE
    by Leo Huberman and Paul M. Sweezy . . . . . . . 115

# PREFACE

Historically, socialism arose as a reaction to the reality of capitalism. Socialist theory was first of all an indictment of capitalism, and the socialist movement aimed to create a society which would overcome or eliminate the horrors and evils which capitalism had brought with it. This explains why we believe that an introduction to socialism, if it is to provide the reader with historical perspective and insight, must focus primarily on capitalism.

There was a period in the late 1940's and 1950's, aptly described by the late C. Wright Mills as the "American Celebration," when it was intellectually fashionable to assume that capitalism had reformed itself. Everything may not have been for the best in the best of all possible worlds, but at any rate that was the trend. Socialism was definitely *passé*, and few took the trouble to familiarize themselves with socialist ideas, programs, and accomplishments. It was during this period that most of the essays and articles assembled in this book were written. Today it is the American Celebration which is *passé*; the horrors and evils of capitalism have never been so obvious or so threatening. We believe that the time has come when the socialist indictment and the socialist alternative should once again receive an attentive and respectful hearing.

Apart from updating figures here and there we have made no substantive changes in what we wrote between 10 and 20 years ago. So far as the indictment of capitalism is concerned —and this is the core of the book—we would not express our views much differently today. It is even an advantage to demonstrate in this practical way that this aspect of socialist doctrine has strong and deep roots and does not require to be revised every few years.

When it comes to the analysis of the socialist alternative in practice—i.e. to the actual performance of the socialist countries—matters are not so simple. Here change has been extraordinarily rapid in the last two decades, and it is now clear that much more experimentation and change are in prospect. Much of what we wrote in this area is therefore inevitably dated. Our hopes led us to be too optimistic about the rapidity with which socialist performance would match socialist theory; we underestimated the time and effort needed to change people's ways of thinking and acting; we did not anticipate the Sino-Soviet split; we did not understand the extent to which the Soviet Union might be a negative as well as a positive example to others, such as the Chinese and the Cubans, seeking to build socialism and take the road to communism.

We could not take account of all these momentous happenings in a brief introduction to socialism, however; and it did not seem appropriate to re-write the relatively few pages, dealing mostly with the Soviet Union, where these matters are touched upon. Instead, we have left these pages as they were written—after all, mistakes can also be instructive if they are recognized as such—and added a new essay written for the November, 1967, issue of MONTHLY REVIEW in which we give our latest, but undoubtedly by no means final, appraisal of the pluses and minuses of socialist performance in the Soviet Union, the oldest of the socialist countries.

LEO HUBERMAN<br>
PAUL M. SWEEZY

*February 12, 1968*

# FREEDOM UNDER CAPITALISM AND SOCIALISM
## BY LEO HUBERMAN

On that never-to-be-forgotten day, the inhabitants of the city were stunned by the pronouncement of a dictator. Some 3500 people, about a quarter of the working population of the city, suddenly learned that they could work until the end of the year and then—no more jobs. The mills were to be closed by order of the dictator.

The moment you hear that word dictator, you probably think of any one of a number of countries, except your own; yet the event I have just described took place here in our own country, in the New England town of Nashua, New Hampshire, U.S.A., whose people have long boasted that theirs is the greatest democracy in the world. Surely there could not be any dictatorship there?

But there was. There was the dictatorship of private ownership of the means of production. There was the dictatorship of Textron, Inc., whose owners, not elected by the people of New Hampshire, responsible to no one but themselves, made a decision affecting the life of every person in the city of Nashua. Concerned only with their own advantage, the owners of Textron decided that they would shut down the mills in Nashua and move South where labor was cheaper—and profits larger.

Many of the 3500 workers in the Nashua Mills had worked all their lives in the textile industry and knew no other trade. What was going to happen to them? That was no concern of Textron.

Few disasters so great as the sudden loss of employment for one quarter of the working people can hit an unsuspecting community. What was going to happen to Nashua? That was no concern of Textron.

---

*This is the Fritz Pappenheim Memorial Lecture, given on May 1, 1965, at Yale University under the auspices of the Yale Socialist Union. It appears here in slightly abbreviated form. The full text appeared in* MONTHLY REVIEW, *October 1965.*

Was it in the interest of the United States of America to have an industry located in one region of the country move to another region? That was no concern of Textron.

In true dictator fashion, with no discussion of the question with the people directly affected, and with no regard for the well-being of the workers, the city, or the nation, Textron had made its decision. Nashua, New Hampshire was to be added to the long list of once thriving cities transformed into a chronically depressed area—by the arbitrary order of a group of absentee owners concerned only with the hunt for profits.

The case of Nashua is a dramatic, but by no means unique, example of the absence of economic government "of the people, by the people, and for the people." The *New York Times*, on March 16, just a month and a half ago, began a dispatch from Yonkers, New York with these words: "The Otis Elevator Company, which is the largest employer in this city, said today it would eliminate from its local payroll 26 percent of the 2100 employees. Efforts of state officials to alter the decision have failed."

The Temporary National Economic Committee of the United States Senate, which characterized the behavior of our economic dictators in time of war as "blackmail," called attention to the fact that our so-called system of "free private enterprise" is not that at all—it is, in fact, largely a system in which economic power is highly concentrated, a system of monopoly, described by TNEC in these words: "A more nearly perfect mechanism for making the poor poorer and the rich richer could scarcely be devised. . . . We know that most of the wealth and income of the country is owned by a few large corporations, that these corporations in turn are owned by an infinitesimally small number of people, and that the profits from the operation of these corporations go to a very small group."

That Senate report was published in 1941 and today, 24 years later, the statistics indicate that the good things of life still flow in a never-ending stream to a small, privileged rich class; while frightening insecurity, degrading poverty, and inequality of opportunity are the lot of the large, unprivileged poor class.

In our "affluent society" 66 million Americans live in

poverty or deprivation. Two weeks ago, on April 20, the *New York Times* ran an editorial citing Welfare Department figures showing that the number of children growing up on the public relief rolls was rising. "The cycle of inherited want in this city is becoming a disastrous upward spiral," said the *Times*. "300,000 New York children are living on public assistance in this most prosperous year in America's history."

At his news conference on April 2, a month ago, President Johnson reported that the unemployment rate in the country had fallen. He said: "Good as it is, 4.7 percent unemployment in our economy is equal to, or greater than, the individual population of at least two thirds of our states. . . . And that many is too many."

On the state of education in the country, the President said:

How many young lives have been wasted; how many entire families now live in misery; how much talent has this great powerful nation lost because America has failed to give all of our children a chance to learn. . . .

Last year almost one out of every three of all draftees were rejected by the armed services because they could not read or write at the eighth grade level. . . . Today as I speak . . . nearly 54 million have not finished high school. This is a shocking waste of human resources.

Right, Mr. President. This is, indeed, a shocking waste of human resources—this poverty, this degradation, this illiteracy, this American way of life, for so many of our people. And equally shocking is the way of life for those whose property, power, and privilege stem from their ownership of the means of production in this capitalist system.

We get a glimpse of what life is like for those on the upper rung of the economic ladder, in an article in the *New York Times* Magazine Section on December 13 of last year—just before Christmas. The article was concerned with the problem of what to give to "those overprivileged people who are apt to be skipped by Santa simply because they have everything. Luckily the plight of the pampered," the author says with tongue in cheek, "has not gone unconsidered by stores with a social conscience."

For the night before Christmas, a man of feeling (and ready cash) might send a lady a sincere bouquet—of red silk roses handmade in Paris, $250 the dozen from Flowers Unlimited. An underweight girl might be even more pleased by Plumbridge's 10-lb. assortment of nourishing candy packed in a Tiffany glass bowl, $350. And, as stuffing for a sheer little stocking, Kent of London's 9-kt. gold-backed brush for furs, $450 (special order) from Saks Fifth Avenue; Arthur King's $10,000 diamond-stoppered perfume bottle carved from a single emerald, and/or Neiman-Marcus's diamond-emerald necklace, a bibelot so dainty it barely whispers its $125,000 price. . . .

To round out the gift picture, there are the warm little things that make a house a home. What can give that special glow to a room better than wall-to-wall mink carpeting? For $600 a square yard, furrier Georges Kaplan is even prepared to install it on Christmas Eve. M. Kaplan has also come up with a practical notion for closets: clothes hangers covered in durable chinchilla, at $175 a piece. To brighten up the children's bathroom, there's Sherle Wagner's jeweled basin set—a pair of 24-kt. gold-plated faucets set with semiprecious malachite, $495.

Now obviously, there must be some method whereby this set of property relations, so advantageous to the few and so disadvantageous to the many, is maintained. There must be some agency with power to see to it that this system of social and economic domination by the wealthy minority over the laboring majority is preserved.

In the conflict between those who have private property in the means of production and those who have not, the haves find in the state an indispensable weapon against the have-nots.

In slave society the state power was used in the interests of the slave owners. In feudal society the state power was used in the interests of the feudal lords and feudal church. In capitalist society the state power is used in the interests of the capitalists.

That the state is a weapon of the ruling class was plain to Adam Smith as long ago as 1776. In his famous book, *The Wealth of Nations,* Smith wrote: "Civil government, so far as it is instituted for the security of property is in reality instituted for the defense of the rich against the poor or of those who have some property against those who have none at all."

The class that rules economically—that owns the means of

production—also rules politically. The form of government makes no difference. Adam Smith, for example, was a native of England which was a monarchy. Here in the United States we never had a king to rule over us. But Samuel Clesson Allen, Massachusetts minister, teacher, and Congressman, from his experience in this democratic republic, came, in the 1830's, to much the same conclusions about the role of the state as did Smith: "What have governments been, and what are they now, but the combinations of the rich and the powerful to increase their riches and extended their power? . . . What have the laboring class to expect from their justice or their charity? What from a government in their control? . . . It is in the nature of things that government will always adapt its policy, be the theory of its constitution what it may, to the interests and aims of the predominating class."

Those members of the laboring class who, unlike Allen, thought of the government as being impartial, as standing above classes, soon learned the facts of life. They found that a government in control of "the rich and the powerful" was bound to make laws which were in the interests of the rich and the powerful.

"Whenever the legislature," observed Adam Smith, "attempts to regulate the differences between masters and their workmen, its counsellors are always the masters."

It is not at all surprising that the law-makers look for counsel to the "masters" of Smith's day—the capitalists of our day. It would be surprising indeed if they didn't, since, by and large, it is the capitalists who put them into their seats of power.

The capitalists pay the campaign funds and therefore they control the election machinery. Seldom is a person nominated, let alone elected, who does not meet with the approval of the men who put up the money to swing the election.

It is true that in a democracy like the United States, the people vote the respective candidates into office. They do have a choice of Democrat X or Republican Y. But that is never a choice between a candidate who is on one side of the class war and a candidate who is on the other side.* There is little basic difference in attitude toward the system of private property relations between the candidates of the major parties. What differences do exist have to do mainly with variation in emphasis or detail—almost never with fundamentals.

Boiled down to its essentials, the freedom to choose between Democrat X or Republican Y means for the workers merely the freedom to choose which particular representative of the capitalist class will make the laws in Congress in the interests of the capitalist class.

In the mind of one of our greatest Americans there was no doubt that the class that ruled economically also ruled politically. "Suppose you go to Washington and try to get at your Government. You will always find that while you are politely listened to, the men really consulted are the men who have the biggest stake—the big bankers, the big manufacturers, the big masters of commerce, the heads of railroad corporations and of steamship corporations. . . . The masters of the Government of the United States are the combined capitalists and manufacturers of the United States."

This very revealing statement was published in 1913 in the book *The New Freedom* by Woodrow Wilson. The author was in a position to know what he was talking about. He was President of the United States at the time.

My own first inkling of the truth of Wilson's observation came in 1932 when I paid an income tax of $24 and I read in the newspaper that J. P. Morgan paid nothing that year. I've been interested in our tax laws ever since—and believe me, much can be learned about democracy in the United States from a careful study of our tax laws. In a speech in the Senate arguing for tax reform on November 1, 1963, Senator Douglas revealed the fact that there were 15 persons with incomes of more than one million dollars, and 5 persons with gross incomes of more

---

* That choice is, of course, offered to the voters by the candidates of some minority parties. But since every powerful organ of propaganda is on the side of Big Business, the likelihood that the people will vote these candidates into office is, in normal times, exceedingly small.

than 5 million dollars "who did not pay a single cent in taxes." These figures, said Senator Douglas, "are shocking when one considers that any worker with a wife and two children who is earning just $100 a week . . . pays about $456 in Federal income taxes."

Understand, I am not suggesting that any of these millionaires who pay no taxes are cheating. On the contrary, my point is that the laws are so designed that they do not have to pay taxes. And if you argue that these cases are not typical, then I commend to your attention an article which appeared in the *New York Times* Magazine Section on April 11, just a few weeks ago, by Senator Gore of Tennessee, entitled "How to be Rich Without Paying Taxes." The Senator says: "Now, when examples like these are brought to light by proponents of tax reform, many people dismiss them as untypical; they still believe that we have a progressive system of taxation based on ability to pay. The truth, however, is that the 'typical' taxpayer with an income of one million dollars or more per year regularly pays a smaller percentage of his income in taxes than do some factory workers or teachers."

Now, just as the state uses its power to protect the interests of the capitalist class inside the country, so it uses its armed force to protect those interests outside the country. Military strength does not come cheap. It costs a lot of money—something like 70 percent of the budget is allocated to pay the expenses of past wars and present "national defense." The money that is essential for adequate housing, community services, health, education, and social welfare is always hard to find but there is always plenty for our military needs. That was what Senator Fulbright pointed out in his speech on the Cold War on April 5, 1964:

There is a most striking paradox in the fact that military budgets of over 50 billion dollars are adopted by the Congress after only perfunctory debate while domestic education and welfare programs involving sums which are mere fractions of the military budget are painstakingly examined and then either considerably reduced or rejected outright.

What Senator Fulbright calls "a most striking paradox" is paradoxical only to those who think of the state as being an impartial agency, above class. To those who recognize that the state is an instrument through which one class establishes its domination over the other class, there is no mystery in the laws made by Congress.

A more pertinent question arises: if the machinery of the state is controlled by the capitalist class and functions in its interest, then how does it ever happen that laws are passed which are of benefit to the working class? How does it ever happen that laws designed to regulate and limit the power of the capitalists ever get on the statute books?

It is true that there are times when such laws are passed. This happened, for example, during the administration of Franklin D. Roosevelt. Why?

The state acts on behalf of the non-owners and against the owners when it is forced to do so. It will yield on this or that particular point of conflict because pressure from the working class is so great that concessions must be made, or "law and order" will be endangered, or worse still (from the point of view of the ruling class) revolution may ensue. But the important point to remember is that whatever concessions are won in such periods are confined to the existing property relations. The framework of the capitalist system itself is left untouched. It is always within that framework that concessions are made. The aim of the ruling class is to yield a part in order to save the whole.

All the gains won by the working class during the administration of President Roosevelt—and they were many—did not change the system of private ownership of the means of production. They did not bring the overthrow of one class by another. When Mr. Roosevelt died, the employers were still in their accustomed places, the workers in theirs. Mr. Roosevelt spoke the truth when he said, three years after he took office: "No one in the United States believes more firmly than I do in the system of private business, private property and private profit. . . . It was this Administration which saved the system of private profit and free enterprise after it had been dragged to the brink of ruin."

# FREEDOM UNDER CAPITALISM AND SOCIALISM

Freedom, for most Americans, means the right to do and say what they please without interference by the state. The guarantees in the Bill of Rights are specific—freedom of religion, freedom of speech, freedom of the press, freedom of assembly, freedom from arbitrary arrest. These are precious liberties. They have been essential weapons in the struggle of the working class to better its conditions.

And Americans have, without doubt, enjoyed these freedoms to a greater extent than have the people of many other countries. Nevertheless, it would be foolish to maintain that the rights guaranteed us in the Constitution always exist in fact. The freedoms which are ours on the books are not always ours in real life.

Thus the House Committee on Un-American Activities vilifies and persecutes citizens in utter disregard of the Bill of Rights.

The FBI is turned into a political police with endless files of secret dossiers on the beliefs and activities of millions of Americans.

The *New York Times* of April 14 reports: "A bid by editors of 13 college newspapers to send student journalists to report stories in Cuba during the Easter vacation has been turned down by the State Department."

Commentators are driven off the air because they are too "liberal"; film and TV writers are blacklisted because of their radical views; members of the Progressive Labor Movement are given jail sentences because of their militancy.

Imprisonment, beatings, torture, and even murder of the heroes, both black and white, who are enlisted in the Negro Freedom Movement, are a common occurrence.

Freedom of the press, with a very few honorable exceptions, has come to mean printing the many lies handed out by government officials with the result that the American people are probably the least informed public in the world on the nature of the terrible happenings in Vietnam.

Freedom of the press is a high-sounding phrase which rings a bell in our ears. We like to think it means the right of free public expression but the Commission on Freedom of the

16  FREEDOM UNDER CAPITALISM AND SOCIALISM

Press, headed by Robert Hutchins, found otherwise: "Protection against government is now not enough to guarantee that a man who has something to say shall have a chance to say it. The owners and managers of the press determine which persons, which facts, which versions of the facts, and which ideas shall reach the public."

The truly noble concept of freedom of the press has been translated by those "owners and managers" into the right to come out bravely and wholeheartedly—for the status quo. This is beautifully illustrated in the headlines in the Paris newspapers reporting the journey of Napoleon across France, on his return from Elba, March 9 to March 22, 1815:

March 9
THE ANTHROPOPHAGUS HAS QUITTED HIS DEN

March 10
THE CORSICAN OGRE HAS LANDED AT CAPE JUAN

March 11
THE TIGER HAS ARRIVED AT CAP

March 12
THE MONSTER SLEPT AT GRENOBLE

March 13
THE TYRANT HAS PASSED THROUGH LYONS

March 14
THE USURPER IS DIRECTING HIS STEPS TOWARD DIJON

March 18
BONAPARTE IS ONLY SIXTY LEAGUES FROM THE CAPITAL
He has been fortunate enough to escape his pursuers

March 19
BONAPARTE IS ADVANCING WITH RAPID STEPS, BUT HE WILL NEVER ENTER PARIS

March 20
NAPOLEON WILL, TOMORROW, BE UNDER OUR RAMPARTS

March 21
THE EMPEROR IS AT FONTAINEBLEAU

March 22
HIS IMPERIAL AND ROYAL MAJESTY
arrvied yesterday evening at the Tuileries, amid the joyful acclamations of his devoted and faithful subjects

We in the United States tend to think that the whole

question of freedom hinges on setting limits to the power of the law to dictate or control what we may say or do. But the absence of coercion, valuable as it undoubtedly is, does not necessarily insure freedom. The mere fact that no law prohibits you from doing something does not mean that you are in a position to do it. You have the right to go to the nearest airport and take a plane to New Orleans, or Chicago, or Hollywood—but you are not really free to do so if you don't have the money to pay for the ticket. Of what use is it to have a right if you are not able to exercise it?

"Necessitous men are not free men," said President Roosevelt in his message to Congress on January 11, 1944. And 20 years later, in his address to the 1964 convention of the Southern Christian Leadership Conference, Dr. Martin Luther King, Jr., echoed that concept in these words:

Of what advantage is it to the Negro to establish that he can be served in integrated restaurants or accommodated in integrated hotels, if he is bound to the kind of financial servitude which will not allow him to take a vacation, or even take his wife out to dinner? What will it profit him to be able to send his children to an integrated school if the family income is insufficient to buy them school clothes?

Freedom, then, means a lot more than mere absence of restraint. It has a positive aspect, which for the majority of the people, is of deeper significance. Freedom means living life to the fullest—the economic ability to satisfy the needs of the body in regard to adequate food, clothing, and shelter, plus effective opportunity to cultivate the mind, develop one's personality, and assert one's individuality.

This concept of freedom will probably come as a surprise to those who have always had the means to satisfy their desires and develop their faculties. For them, freedom is measured solely in terms of non-interference with their rights—free elections, free speech, free press; for the vast majority of mankind, however, freedom is measured less in terms of rights and more in terms of bread, leisure, security.

It is the failure to understand this fundamental fact which makes the revolutionary upheavals of our time incomprehensible to so many Americans. Let me repeat: I do not, for one moment, minimize the value of free elections, free speech, and free press.

These are valuable, essential liberties, of the utmost importance to people who have enough to eat, decent housing, education, and medical care. But they are not of particular urgency to hungry, uneducated, diseased, exploited people. When those of us with full bellies tell the people with empty bellies that what they need most in the world is free elections, they will not listen; they know better, they know that what they need first and foremost is bread, shoes, a school for their children, medical care, adequate clothing, a decent home. All these necessities of life, plus the dignity that goes with their enjoyment is what spells freedom to them.

Here is a simple test by which you can establish the validity of this broader concept of freedom. Ask yourself these questions:

Is a jobless man who is starving, free?

Is a man in constant fear of losing his job, free?

Is an illiterate ignorant person, shut off from the world of books and culture, free?

Is a talented person, unable to afford the schooling which would help his talent flourish, free?

In capitalist society, only the rich are able to enjoy freedom in its broader sense of abundance, security, leisure. The poor are not free. Nor can they win their freedom under capitalism. The only way to rid society of that invisible dictatorship whose mere existence makes all fine talk of freedom so much nonsense —the dictatorship exercised by the owners of the means of production—is to substitute collective for private ownership; to establish socialism in place of capitalism.

The structure of the capitalist system makes the attainment of genuine freedom impossible; the structure of the socialist system makes genuine freedom possible.

Socialism will not bring perfection. It will not create a paradise. It will not solve all the problems that face mankind. Socialism will solve only those problems which can be solved at this particular stage in the development of man.

The conscious planned development of the commonly-owned productive forces will enable socialist society to attain a far higher level of production than was possible under capitalism. In place of the economic disorder which arises in capitalist society when each separate owner of the means of production does as he pleases when he pleases, the socialist government substitutes order through organized effort and plan. Instead of private production for profit, planned production for use. That a planned socialist society is much more efficient than chaotic capitalism in all matters having to do with man's utilization of his material environment is sufficiently clear in the progress already evident in the Soviet Union.

But economic and technological success is only part of the socialist dream. The great socialists of the past have always thought of the good society as not only rationally planned but also democratically controlled—a society of cooperation and brotherhood in which no small group monopolizes power or enjoys special privileges; in which all citizens have the right to be fully informed, to make up their own minds, to dissent and to criticize and, most important of all, to participate actively in making and carrying out the decisions that control their lives.

Judged by this standard the Soviet Union still has most of the road to travel—it is not yet a good society. Though it has made notable advances in recent years, it is still far from democracy.

Many good reasons have been advanced for the lack of democracy in the Soviet Union and it may be that complete democracy will be unobtainable there until the socialist prophesy of the withering away of the State comes true. That was, indeed, Lenin's view: "While the State exists, there can be no freedom; when freedom comes there will be no State." But already the absence of open discussion and debate, the failure to develop democratic institutions and procedures in the Soviet Union have become the target of criticism not only from the Soviet masses, but also from within the top leadership of the Communist international movement. It may be that Togliatti, the leader of the Italian Communist Party, was charting the future in his famous Testament of last winter when he attacked "the regime of restrictions and suppression of democratic and personal freedom introduced by Stalin" and called for a return to "a wide liberty of expression and debate on culture, art, and also on politics."

But there are no guarantees that the desired political freedoms will be added to economic freedom attainable under socialism. On September 6, 1880, the *New York Sun* printed an interview which John Swinton, famous American journalist, had with Karl Marx. The interview ends with these words:

During an interspace of silence, I interrupted the revolutionist and philosopher in these fateful words: "What is?"
In deep and solemn tone, he replied, "Struggle."
At first it seemed as though I had heard the echo of despair; but peradventure, it was the law of life.

The moral, it seems to me, is plain. First we must fight to win socialism; then we must fight to make it fulfill its promise. In short, struggle never ends. It is the law of life.

In his brilliant essay, "The Commitment of the Intellectual" my friend, the late Professor Paul Baran, defines an intellectual as "in essence a social critic, a person whose concern is to identify, to analyze, and in this way to help overcome the obstacles barring the way to the attainment of a better, more humane, and more rational social order."

Baran points out that it is not easy for the intellectual to stand up to the pressures brought on him to surrender to the ideology of the ruling class. It takes intellectual courage—much more rare than physical bravery.

There are students in this audience who knew Fritz Pappenheim. They know that he was one of the rare ones—a sweet gentle person, a profound scholar who had the courage to be an intellectual. We honor his memory.

# THE ABC OF SOCIALISM
BY LEO HUBERMAN

The only thing most Americans know about socialism is that they don't like it. They have been led to believe that socialism is something to be either ridiculed as impractical, or feared as an instrument of the devil.

This is a disturbing situation. It is a mistake to dismiss or condemn so important a subject on the basis of the extremely superficial and biased accounts of it which are now so widespread in the United States. Socialism is a world-wide movement. The millions who hate it in this country are matched by millions in other countries who rejoice in it. No idea has ever caught the imagination of so many people in so short a time.

Socialism has already become the way of life for some 200,000,000 people—the inhabitants of one-sixth of the earth's surface. It is fast becoming the way of life for an additional 600,000,000 people. These two groups together make up approximately one-third of the earth's population.

It is deplorable, therefore, that socialism for many Americans is nothing more than a dirty word. Whether it be good or evil, whether it should be fought against or striven for, it must first be understood. To help achieve that understanding is the purpose of this pamphlet.

The first half outlines the socialist economic analysis of capitalism—its structure and its defects—with particular reference to the United States today. The second half deals with the theory of socialism—with its greatest thinkers and what they taught. By far the most important and influential figures in the development of basic socialist doctrine were Karl Marx and Friedrich Engels. It is their concept of socialism which has lived and is today the foundation stone of the movement on every continent—and which forms the basis for this pamphlet.

A word of warning. The picture as we present it, is unvarnished and stark. It will dismay some readers, anger others. That is to be

---

*The material presented here was condensed from Leo Huberman's book,* The Truth About Socialism, *and edited by Sybil H. May.*

expected. To have one's attitudes and beliefs challenged in so direct a fashion is always a shock. The wise reader, therefore, will read through the whole pamphlet before coming to any definite conclusions about socialist philosophy.

Finally, it should be remembered that this pamphlet is an introduction to socialism, a sketch of its main outlines, nothing more. The literature on the subject is vast; interested readers should not stop with this elementary A-B-C but go on to the many other works which treat the topic with the thoroughness it deserves.

# PART I ... SOCIALIST ANALYSIS OF CAPITALISM

## 1. CLASS STRUGGLE

No matter whether they're rich or poor, strong or weak, white, black, yellow, or brown, people everywhere must produce and distribute the things they need in order to live.

The system of production and distribution in the United States is called *capitalism*. Many other countries of the world have the same system.

In order to produce and distribute bread, clothes, houses, autos, radios, newspapers, medicines, schools, this, that, and the other thing, you have to have two essentials:

1. Land, mines, raw materials, machines, factories—what economists call the "means of production."
2. Labor—workers who use their strength and skill on and with the means of production to turn out the required goods.

In the United States, as in other capitalist countries, the means of production are not public property. The land, raw materials, factories, machines, are owned by individuals—by capitalists. That is a fact of tremendous importance. Because whether you do or do not own the means of production determines your position in society. If you belong to the small group of owners of the means of production—the capitalist class—you can live without working. If you belong to the large group that does not own the means of production—the working class—you can't live unless you work.

One class lives by owning; the other class lives by working. The capitalist class gets its income by employing other people to work for it; the working class gets its income in the form of wages for the work it does.

Since labor is essential to the production of goods we need in order to live, you would suppose that those who do the labor—the working class—would be handsomely rewarded. But they aren't. In capitalist society, it isn't those who *work* the most who get the largest incomes, it is those who *own* the most.

Profit makes the wheels go round in capitalist society. The smart business man is the one who pays as little as possible for what he buys and receives as much as possible for what he sells. The first step on the road to high profits is to reduce expenses. One of the expenses of production is wages to labor. It is therefore to the interest of the employer to pay as low wages as possible. It is likewise to his interest to get as much work out of his laborers as possible.

The interests of the owners of the means of production and of the men who work for them are opposed. For the capitalists, property takes first place, humanity second place; for the workers, humanity—themselves—takes first place, property second place. That is why, in capitalist society, there is always conflict between the two classes.

Both sides in the class war act the way they do because they must. The capitalist must try to make profits to remain a capitalist. The worker must try to get decent wages to remain alive. Each can succeed only at the expense of the other.

All the talk about "harmony" between capital and labor is nonsense. In capitalist society there can be no such harmony because what is good for one class is bad for the other, and vice versa.

The relationship, then, that *must* exist between the owners of the means of production and the workers in capitalist society is the relationship of a knife to a throat.

## 2. SURPLUS VALUE

In capitalist society, man does not produce things which he wants to satisfy his own needs, he produces things to sell to others. Where formerly people produced *goods for their own use,* today they produce *commodities for the market.*

The capitalist system is concerned with the production and exchange of commodities.

The worker does not own the means of production. He can make his living in only one way—by hiring himself out for wages to those who do. He goes to market with a commodity for sale—his capacity to work, his labor power. That's what the employer buys from him. That's what the employer pays him wages for. The worker sells his commodity, labor power, to the boss in return for wages.

How much wages will he get? What is it that determines the rate of his wages?

The key to the answer is found in the fact that what the

## SOCIALIST ANALYSIS OF CAPITALISM 25

worker has to sell is a commodity. The value of his labor power, like that of any other commodity, is determined by the amount of socially necessary labor time required to produce it. But since the worker's labor power is part of himself, the value of his labor power is equal to the food, clothing, and shelter necessary for him to live (and since the supply of labor must continue, to raise a family).

In other words, if the owner of a factory, mill, or mine wants forty hours of labor done, he must pay the man who is to do the work enough to live on, and to bring up children capable of taking his place when he gets too old to work, or dies.

Workers will get then, in return for their labor power, subsistence wages, with enough more (in some countries) to enable them to buy a radio, or an electric refrigerator, or a ticket to the movies occasionally.

Does this economic law that workers' wages will tend to be merely subsistence wages mean that political and trade union action by workers is useless? No, it definitely does not. On the contrary, workers, through their unions, have been able in some countries, including the United States, to raise wages above the minimum subsistence level. And the important point to remember is that this is the *only* way open to workers to keep that economic law from operating all the time.

Where does profit come from?

It is not in the process of exchange of commodities but rather in the process of production that we will find the answer. The profits that go to the capitalist class arise out of production.

The workers by transforming raw material into the finished article have brought new wealth into existence, have created a new value. The difference between what the worker is paid in wages and the amount of value he has added to the raw material is what the employer keeps.

That's where his profit comes from.

When a worker hires himself out to an employer he doesn't sell him what he produces; the worker sells his ability to produce.

The employer does not pay the worker for the product of eight hours work; the employer pays him to work eight hours.

The worker sells his labor power for the length of the whole working day—say eight hours. Now suppose the time necessary to produce the value of the worker's wages is four hours. He doesn't stop working then and go home. Oh, no. He has been hired to work eight hours. So he continues to work the other four hours. In these four hours, he is working *not for himself,* but *for his employer.* Part of his labor is *paid* labor; part is *unpaid* labor. The employer's profit comes from the unpaid labor.

There *must* be a difference between what the worker is paid and the value of what he produces, else the employer wouldn't hire him. The difference between what the worker receives in wages and the value of the commodity he produces is called *surplus value.*

Surplus value is the profit that goes to the employer. He buys labor power at one price and sells the product of labor at a higher price. The difference—surplus value—he keeps for himself.

## 3. ACCUMULATION OF CAPITAL

The capitalist begins with money. He buys the means of production and labor power. The workers, using their labor power on the means of production, produce commodities. The capitalist takes these commodities and sells them—for money. The amount of money he gets at the end of the process must be greater than the amount of money he started with. The difference is his profit.

If the amount of money at the end of the process is not greater than the amount of money he started with, then there is no profit and he stops producing. Capitalist production does not begin or end with people's needs. It begins and ends with money.

Money cannot become more money by standing still, by being hoarded. It can only grow by being used as capital, that is by buying the means of production and labor power and thus getting a share of the new wealth created by workers every hour of every day of every year.

It's a real merry-go-round. The capitalist seeks more and more profits so he can accumulate more capital (means of production and labor power), so he can make more and more profits, so he can accumulate more capital, so he can etc., etc., etc.

Now the way to increase profits is to get the workers to turn out more and more goods faster and faster at less and less cost.

Good idea, but how to do it? Machines and scientific management, that was (and is) the answer. Greater division of labor. Mass production. Speed-up. Greater efficiency in the plant. More machines. Power-driven machines that enable one worker to produce as much as five did before, as much as ten did, eighteen, twenty-seven. . . .

The workers who are made "superfluous" by machinery become an "industrial reserve army" which can slowly starve, or, by its very existence, help to force down the wages of those who are lucky enough to have jobs.

And not only do machines create a surplus population of workers, they also change the character of labor. Unskilled, low-paid labor—with a machine—can do work that required skilled high-paid labor before. Children can take the place of adults in the factory, women can replace men.

Competition forces each capitalist to look for ways whereby he can produce goods more cheaply than others. The lower his "unit labor cost" the more possible it is to undersell his competitors and still make a profit. With the extension of the use of machinery, the capitalist is able to get the workers to produce more and more goods faster and faster at less and less cost.

But the new and improved machinery which makes this possible costs a lot of money. It means production on a larger scale than before, it means bigger and bigger factories. In other words, it means the accumulation of more and more capital.

There is no choice for the capitalist. The greatest amount of profits goes to the capitalist who uses the most advanced and efficient technical methods. So all capitalists keep striving for improvements. But these improvements require more and more capital. To stay in business at all, to meet the competition of others and preserve what he has, the capitalist must keep constantly expanding his capital.

Not only does he *want* more profits so he can accumulate more capital so he can make more profits—he finds that he is *forced* to do so by the system.

## 4. MONOPOLY

One of the greatest hoaxes ever perpetrated on the American people is the ever-repeated assertion that our economic system is one of "free private enterprise."

That is not true. Only *part* of our economic system is competitive, free, and individualistic. The remainder—and by far the most important part—is the exact opposite: monopolized, controlled, and collectivistic.

Competition, according to theory, was a fine thing. But capitalists found that practice didn't jibe with theory. They found that competition lessened profits while combination increased profits. They were interested in profits so why compete? It was better—from their point of view—to combine.

And combine they did—in oil, sugar, whiskey, iron, steel, coal, and a host of other commodities.

"Free competitive enterprise" was already on its way out as far back as 1875. By 1888 trusts and monopolies had such a stranglehold on American economic life that President Grover Cleveland felt it necessary to sound a warning to Congress: "As we view the achievements of aggregated capital, we discover the existence of trusts, combinations, and monopolies, while the citizen is struggling far in the rear or is trampled to death beneath an iron heel. Corporations, which should be carefully restrained creatures of the law and the servants of the people, are fast becoming the people's masters."

Through the marriage of industrial and finance capital, some corporations were able to expand to so great an extent that in some industries today a handful of firms, literally, produce more than half the total output or nearly all of it. In these industries, certainly, the "traditional American system of free competitive enterprise" no longer exists. In its place there is concentration of economic power in a few hands—monopoly.

Here are some specific examples from the 1946 report of the House of Representatives' Committee on Small Business, entitled *United States Versus Economic Concentration and Monopoly*:

General Motors, Chrysler, and Ford together produce nine out of every ten cars made in the United States.

In 1934 the Big Four tobacco companies—American Tobacco Company, R. J. Reynolds, Liggett & Myers, and P. Lorillard—"produced 84 per cent of the cigarettes, 74 per cent of the smoking tobacco, and 70 per cent of the chewing tobacco."

The Big Four rubber companies—Goodyear, Firestone, U. S. Rubber, and Goodrich—account for "nearly 93 per cent of the total net sales of the rubber industry."

Before the war, the three largest companies in the soap industry—Proctor & Gamble, Lever Bros., and Colgate-Palmolive-Peet Co., controlled 80 per cent of the business. Another 10 per cent was secured by three other companies. The remaining 10 per cent was distributed among approximately 1,200 soap producers.

Two companies—Libby-Owens-Ford and the Pittsburgh Plate Glass Co.—together make 95 per cent of all plate glass in the country.

The United States Shoe Machinery Co. controls more than 95 per cent of the entire shoe-machinery business in the United States.

It is not difficult to see that with such extensive domination, the monopoly capitalists are in a position to fix prices. And they do. They fix them at that point where they can make the highest profits. They fix them by agreement among themselves; or by the most powerful corporation announcing the price and the rest of the industry playing the game of "follow the leader;" or, as frequently happens, they control basic patents and give licenses to produce only to those who agree to stay in line.

Monopoly makes it possible for the monopolists to accomplish their purpose—make tremendous profits. Competitive industries make profits in good times and show deficits in bad times. But for monopoly industries the pattern is different—they make tremendous profits in good times, and some profits in bad times.

The agitation against monopoly power and profits which began in the last quarter of the 19th century continued into the 20th century. But though much was said about the "growing evil," little was done about it. Neither the Federal Trade Commission nor the anti-trust division of the Department of Justice, even when they had the will to do something, was given the funds or the staff to do it with.

As a matter of fact, little could be done about it. When the Standard Oil Company was "dissolved" in 1911, Mr. J. P. Morgan is reported to have made this appropriate comment: "No law can make a man compete with himself." Subsequent events proved Mr. Morgan right. By 1935:

> One-tenth of one per cent of all the corporations in the United States owned 52 per cent of the assets of all of them.
>
> One-tenth of one per cent of all the corporations earned 50 per cent of the net income of all of them.
>
> Less than 4 per cent of all the manufacturing corporations earned 84 per cent of the net profits of all of them.

"A more nearly perfect mechanism for making the poor poorer and the rich richer could scarcely be devised."

That's what the TNEC report says about monopoly.

It gives as evidence the effect of monopoly on workers, producers of materials, consumers, and stockholders.

The workers are made poorer by "the monopolist's failure to pay wages equal to their productivity."

The producers of materials (e.g. farmers) are made poorer by "the low prices that the monopolist sometimes pays."

The consumers are made poorer by "the high prices that the monopolist charges."

The stockholders, on the other hand, are made richer by "the unnecessarily high profits that the monopolist thus obtains."

Whenever the charge is made that there is a dangerous concentration of power and wealth in the hands of a few, the apologists for Big Business deny that the picture is as black as it is painted. They argue that even where there are unnecessarily high profits, these profits are distributed to millions of people and not to a small group. They argue that there is a wide distribution of stock ownership, that not Mr. Big alone, but Tom, Dick, and Harry and millions of other little fellows own stock in the giant monopoly corporations. It's a plausible argument and it fools a great many people.

But the argument that "the people" own American industry is phony. The number of stockholders in any company may indeed be large. But that is not significant. What is significant is *how many own how much*. What is significant is how the profits are divided among the shareholders. And the moment you get that figure, you find that "the people" as a body own a microscopic share of American industry, while a handful of Big Boys own most of it and reap the colossal profits.

The most impressive and most easily understood figures in this connection were those given to Congress in 1938 by President Roosevelt:

> The year 1929 was a banner year for distribution of stock ownership. But in that year three-tenths of one per cent of our population received 78 per cent of the dividends reported by individuals. This has roughly the same effect as if, out of every 300 persons in our population, one person received 78 cents out of every dollar of corporate dividends while the other 299 persons divided up the other 22 cents between them.

The true picture was presented to Congress in 1941 by Senator O'Mahoney in the Final Report and Recommendations of the Temporary National Economic Committee, of which he was chairman: "We know that most of the wealth and income of the country is owned by a few large corporations, that these corporations in turn are owned by an infinitesimally small number of people and that the profits from the operation of these corporations go to a very small group."

## 5. DISTRIBUTION OF INCOME

It is not true that we Americans live well. The truth is that while a fortunate few of our countrymen live luxuriously, *most* Americans live miserably. The truth is that "our high standard of living" is an empty boast—it does not pertain to most of our people.

President Roosevelt broke through the mist of lies about our high standard of living in his second inaugural address when he said: "I see one-third of a nation ill-housed, ill-clad, ill-nourished."

In the United States, as in all other capitalist countries, there has been a continual increase over the years in the amount of goods and services produced. A never-ending stream of remarkably useful conveniences and incredibly wonderful luxuries has been made available to the people.

However, the availability of this profusion of goods is measured not by the people's needs but by their ability to pay. And the proportion of the national income that goes to most Americans is too small to enable them to purchase the things which would make their lives richer and more satisfying.

Government statistics prove the point. Here, for example, is a table of income distribution by families for the United States in 1966, put out by the Bureau of the Census, *Current Population Reports* (Series P-60, No. 53, 1967, p. 1):

| Total family money income | Number of families |
|---|---|
| Under $1,000 | 1,149,000 |
| $1,000 to $1,999 | 2,635,000 |
| $2,000 to $2,999 | 3,197,000 |
| $3,000 to $3,999 | 3,341,000 |
| $4,000 to $4,999 | 3,474,000 |
| $5,000 to $5,999 | 4,108,000 |
| $6,000 to $6,999 | 4,574,000 |
| $7,000 to $7,999 | 4,542,000 |
| $8,000 to $9,999 | 7,408,000 |
| $10,000 to $14,999 | 10,008,000 |
| $15,000 and over | 4,486,000 |
| Total | 48,922,000 |

Note that some 10,322,000 families, or over 21 per cent of the total, had incomes in 1966 of less than $3,999 for a year! This means that *one out of every five families in the United States had less than $80 per week* to eat, drink, and be merry on. You know how far $80 a week would take a family with the prices prevailing in 1966.

But we don't need to guess. The fact that there are large numbers of desperately poor people in today's "affluent" America was proven by President Johnson himself in his message to Congress in the spring of 1967. He reported that: (1) 60 per cent of all poor children—three out of every five—never see a dentist, in affluent America; (2) 60 per cent of all poor children with disabling handicaps do not receive medical care, in affluent America; (3) In their first year of life, the death rate of poor babies is 50 per cent higher than that of those who are not poor, in affluent America.

While many Americans did not get enough money to live decently, those at the top got much more than enough. In 1966, according to the *Current Population Reports* (p. 7) of the Bureau of Census, the 20 per cent of families at the top of the income ladder received 40.7 per cent of the total income of all of the nation's families, while the 60 per cent of the families at the bottom of the ladder received only 35.5 per cent. The $\frac{1}{5}$ at the top received more income than the $\frac{3}{5}$ at the bottom. But wouldn't the very rich at the top have to pay very high taxes which would take most of their money? That's what they say, but it isn't true.

Not according to an article by Senator Gore of Tennessee which appeared in *The New York Times Magazine* on April 11, 1965. In that article, entitled "How To Be Rich Without Paying Taxes," the Senator says: ". . . Now, when examples like these are brought to light by proponents of tax reform, many people dismiss them as untypical; they still believe that we have a progressive system of taxation based on ability to pay. The truth, however, is that the 'typical' taxpayer with an income of one million dollars or more per year regularly pays a smaller percentage of his income in taxes than do some factory workers or teachers."

It is true that relative to the inhabitants of most other countries, our people, as a whole, have a higher standard of living. But that means, not that we are well off, but that the others are worse off. It doesn't mean what the propagandists want us to believe when they talk about the American "high standard of living."

## 6. CRISIS AND DEPRESSION

The facts about the distribution (or rather, the maldistribution) of income reveal the basic weakness of the capitalist system in its economic aspect.

The income of the mass of people is ordinarily too small to consume the product of industry.

# SOCIALIST ANALYSIS OF CAPITALISM

The income of the wealthy is frequently too large for profitable investment in a market so limited by the poverty of the many.

The bulk of the population which would like to buy doesn't have the money. The few who have the money have so much they can't possibly spend it all.

The expansion of industry has leaped forward on seven-league boots; the expansion of consumer purchasing power has dragged along at a snail's pace.

The problem of mass production is solved; the problem of mass sales of the goods produced is not solved.

The market for goods exists in terms of workers' needs; it does not exist in terms of their ability to pay for the goods they need.

The result is those periodic breakdowns of the system which we call crisis and depression.

*To obtain profits, the capitalist must pay as little as possible to his workers.*

*To sell his products, the capitalist must pay as much as possible to his workers.*

He can't do both.

Low wages make high profits possible, but at the same time they make profits impossible because they reduce the demand for goods.

Insoluble contradiction.

Within the framework of the capitalist system, there is no way out. *We must have depressions.*

After the crisis of 1929, it seemed that the United States had left behind it forever the period when capitalism could still expand. Henceforth it was to be concerned not with generating expansion but with keeping contraction to a minimum.

The people wanted jobs. Their chances of getting them were slim. According to J. M. Keynes, the famous English economist, "The evidence indicates that full, or even approximately full employment, is of rare and shortlived occurrence."

There was, however, one way in which the capitalist system could provide jobs. There was one way in which the paralyzing defects of capitalism—underconsumption and overproduction—could be overcome. There was one way by which the overhanging fear of surplus could be dispelled—one way in which everything that was produced could be sold at a profit.

There was a cure for capitalism's fatal disease of crisis and depression.

WAR.

After 1929, it became apparent that only in the preparation and conduct of a war could the capitalist system be operated so as to provide full employment for men, materials, machinery, and money.

## 7. IMPERIALISM AND WAR

Large scale monopoly industry brought with it greater development of the productive forces than ever before. The power of industrialists to produce goods grew at a more rapid rate than the power of their countrymen to consume them.

That meant they had to sell goods outside the home country. They *had* to find foreign markets which would absorb their surplus manufactures.

Where to find them?

There was one answer—colonies.

The necessity for finding markets for surplus manufactured goods was only one part of the pressure for colonies. Large scale mass production needs vast supplies of raw materials. Rubber, oil, nitrates, tin, copper, nickel—these, and a host of others, were raw materials which were necessary to monopoly capitalists everywhere. They wanted to own or control the sources of those necessary raw materials. This was a second factor making for imperialism.

But more important than either of these pressures was the necessity for finding a market for another surplus—the surplus of capital.

This was the major cause of imperialism.

Monopoly industry brought huge profits to its owners. Super-profits. More money than the owners knew what to do with. More money than they could possibly spend. More money than they could find an outlet for in income-creating investment at home. An over-accumulation of capital.

This alliance of industry and finance seeking profits in markets for goods and capital was the mainspring of imperialism. So J. A. Hobson thought, back in 1902, when he published his pioneer study on the subject: "Imperialism is the endeavor of the great controllers of industry to broaden the channel for the flow of their surplus wealth by seeking foreign markets and foreign investments to take off the goods and capital they cannot sell or use at home."

The treatment of colonial peoples varied from time to time and from place to place. But the atrocities were general—no imperialist nation had clean hands. Leonard Woolf, an acknowledged expert on the subject wrote: "Just as in national society in Europe there have appeared in the last century clearly defined classes, capitalists and workers, exploiters and exploited, so too in international society there have appeared clearly defined classes, the imperialist Powers of the West and the subject races of Africa and the East, the one ruling and exploiting, the other ruled and exploited."

As with other imperialist nations, so with the United States. The profits from all the private investments went to the financial groups involved, but government policy, government money, and government force were employed to make available and to safeguard their private ventures. President Taft was frank about the tie-up that existed between monopoly capitalist necessity and government policy. "While our foreign policy should not be turned a hair's breadth from the straight path of justice, it may well be made to include active intervention to secure for our merchandise and our capitalists opportunity for profitable investment."

In the 20th century, in every great industrial nation, monopoly capitalism grew, and with it the problem of what to do with surplus capital and surplus products. When the various giants in control of their own national markets met on the international markets there was, first, competition—long, hard, bitter. And then, agreements, associations, cartels, on an international basis.

With these huge international combines making arrangements for parcelling out the world market, it would seem that competition must cease and a period of lasting peace begin. But that does not happen, because the strength relations are constantly changing. Some companies grow larger and more powerful, while others decline. Thus what was a fair division at one moment becomes unfair later. There is discontent on the part of the stronger group and a struggle for a larger quota follows. Each government springs to the defense of its own nationals. The inevitable result is war.

Imperialism leads to war. But war doesn't settle anything permanently. The hostilities which can no longer be resolved by bargaining round a table do not disappear because the bargaining is done with the arguments of high explosives, atom bombs, maimed men, and mutilated corpses.

No. The hunt for markets must go on. Monopoly capitalism must have its outlet for surplus goods and capital and new wars will continue to be fought so long as monopoly capitalism continues to exist.

## 8. THE STATE

Private property in the means of production is a special kind of property. It gives to the possessing class power over the non-possessing class. It enables those who own, not only to live without working, but also to determine whether the non-owners shall work and under what conditions. It establishes a master and servant relationship, with the capitalist class in the position of giving orders and the working class in the position of having to obey them.

Understandably, then, there is a perpetual conflict between the two classes.

The capitalist class, through its exploitation of the working class, is handsomely rewarded with wealth, power, and prestige, while the working class is plagued with insecurity, poverty, miserable living conditions.

Now, obviously, there must be some method whereby this set of property relations—so advantageous to the few and so disadvantageous to the many—is maintained. There must be some agency with power to see to it that this system of social and economic domination by the wealthy minority over the laboring majority is preserved.

There is such an agency. It is the state.

It is the function of the state to protect and preserve the set of private property relations which enables the capitalist class to dominate the working class.

It is the function of the state to uphold the system of oppression of one class by another.

In the conflict between those who have private property in the means of production and those who have not, the haves find in the state an indispensable weapon against the have-nots.

We are led to believe that the state is above class—that the government represents all the people, the rich and the poor, the high and the low. But actually, since capitalist society is based on private property, it follows that any attack on private property will be met with the resistance of the state, carried to the length of violence if necessary.

In effect, therefore, so long as classes exist, the state cannot be above class—it must be on the side of the rulers. That the state is a weapon of the ruling class was plain to Adam Smith as long ago as 1776. In his famous book, *The Wealth of Nations,* Smith wrote: "Civil government, so far as it is instituted for the security of property, is in reality instituted for the defense of the rich against the poor, or of those who have some property against those who have none at all."

The class that rules economically—that owns the means of production—also rules politically.

It is true that in a democracy like the United States, the people vote the respective candidates into office. They do have a choice of Democrat X or Republican Y. But that is never a choice between a candidate who is on one side of the class war and a candidate who is on the other side. There is little basic difference in attitude toward the system of private property relations between the candidates of the major parties. What differences do exist have to do mainly with variation in emphasis or detail—almost never with fundamentals.

Boiled down to its essentials, the freedom to choose between Democrat X or Republican Y means for the workers merely the freedom to choose which particular representative of the capitalist class will make the laws in Congress in the interests of the capitalist class.

The tie-up that exists between the men who make the laws and the men in whose interests those laws are made is so close that there can be no doubt of the relationship between the state and the ruling class. In the mind of one of our greatest Americans there was no doubt that the class that ruled economically also ruled politically:

> Suppose you go to Washington and try to get at your Government. You will always find that while you are politely listened to, the men really consulted are the men who have the biggest stake—the big bankers, the big manufacturers, the big masters of commerce, the heads of railroad corporations and of steamship corporations. . . . The masters of the Government of the United States are the combined capitalists and manufacturers of the United States.

This very revealing statement was published in 1913 in a book by Woodrow Wilson. The author was in a position to know what he was talking about. He was President of the United States at the time.

The question arises: if the machinery of the state is controlled by the capitalist class and functions in their interest, then how does it ever happen that laws designed to regulate and limit the power of the capitalists ever get on the statute books?

This happened, for example, during the administration of Franklin D. Roosevelt. Why?

The state acts on behalf of the non-owners and against the owners when it is forced to do so. It will yield on this or that particular point of conflict because pressure from the working class is so great that concessions *must* be made, or "law and order" will be endangered, or worse still (from the point of view of the ruling class) revolution may ensue. But the important point to remember is that whatever concessions are won in such periods are confined to the existing property relations. The framework of the capitalist system itself is left untouched. It is always within that framework that concessions are made. The aim of the ruling class is to yield a part in order to save the whole.

All the gains won by the working class during the administration of President Roosevelt—and they were many—did not change the system of private ownership of the means of production. They did not bring the overthrow of one class by another. When Mr. Roosevelt died, the employers were still in their accustomed places, the workers in theirs.

Since the state is the instrument through which one class establishes and maintains its domination over the other class, genuine freedom for the oppressed majority cannot truly exist. Greater or lesser degrees of freedom—depending on the circumstances—will be granted, but in the last analysis, the words "freedom" and the "state" cannot be combined in a class society.

The state exists to enforce the decisions of the class that controls the government. In capitalist society the state enforces the decisions of the capitalist class. Those decisions are designed to maintain the capitalist system in which the working class must labor in the service of the owners of the means of production.

# PART II ... SOCIALIST INDICTMENT OF CAPITALISM

## 9. CAPITALISM IS INEFFICIENT AND WASTEFUL

The increase in man's power to produce should have resulted in the abolition of want and poverty. It has not had that result—even in the United States, the strongest, richest, and most productive capitalist country in the world.

In the United States, as in every other capitalist country, there is starvation in the midst of plenty, scarcity in the midst of abundance, destitution in the midst of riches.

There must be something fundamentally wrong with an economic system characterized by such contradictions.

There is something wrong. The capitalist system is inefficient and wasteful, irrational, and unjust.

It is inefficient and wasteful because even in those years when it is functioning at its best, one-fifth of its productive mechanism is not in use.

It is inefficient and wasteful because periodically it breaks down—and then, not one-fifth but one-half of its productive capacity is idle. According to Brookings Institution, "At the height of the boom period the amount of idle capacity, expressed in terms of a generalized figure, was something like 20 per cent. In periods of depression this percentage is, of course, very greatly increased—rising as high as 50 per cent in the current [1930's] depression."

It is inefficient and wasteful because it does not always provide useful work for all those who want to work—at the same time that it allows thousands of physically and mentally able persons to live without working.

It is inefficient and wasteful in the employment of a host of advertisers, salesmen, agents, canvassers, and the like, not in the sane production and distribution of goods, but in the insane competition for customers to buy the same commodity from Company A instead of from Company B, or Companies C, D, E, or F.

It is inefficient and wasteful because much of its men and materials is devoted to the production of the most extravagant luxuries at the same time that enough of the necessities of life for all is not produced.

It is inefficient and wasteful because, in its concern for increased price and profitability instead of for human needs, it sanctions the deliberate destruction of crops and goods.

Finally, it is inefficient and wasteful because periodically it leads to war—the merciless diabolical destroyer of all that is good in life, as well as of life itself.

This inefficiency and waste is not merely an abuse which can be corrected. It is part and parcel of the capitalist system. It must continue as long as the system lasts.

During the depression of the 1930's in the United States there were years in which as many as one-fourth of all employable workers who were willing and wanted to work could not find jobs. They starved, or went on home relief, or found make-work jobs with public works agencies. Men, women, and children in every city on bread lines. The magnitude of this waste of labor power is outlined in this never-to-be-forgotten picture: "If all the eleven million unemployed men and women were lined up in one long bread line, standing just close enough for one man to be able to lay his hand on the shoulder of the one in front, that line would extend from New York to Chicago, to St. Louis, to Salt Lake City, yes, to San Francisco. And that's not all. It would extend all the way back again —twice the distance across the continent."

And at the same time that these millions of wretched human beings were in dire need of an opportunity to put their talent and energy to use so they might obtain the bare necessities of life, other more favored men and women who had never known and had no desire to learn what work was, were living in comfort and luxury through their ownership of the means of production. They could live in shameless idleness because the capitalist system was so designed as to enable them to receive an income from the ownership of shares in industries of which they may have never even heard. The poverty of the many who wanted work but could not find it was rendered all the more humiliating because of the riches of the few who were receiving dividends without work.

Confronted with the paradox of poverty in plenty, the capitalist system devises a plan for tackling the problem.

The plan is to abolish the plenty.

Kerosene is poured on potatoes to make them unfit for human consumption, 30 per cent of the coffee crop is destroyed, milk is poured into rivers, fruit is left to rot on the ground.

This seeming insanity is not as crazy at it appears—not in the capitalist system. In an economy which is concerned not with feeding people the potatoes, coffee, milk, and fruit which they need, but only with getting as high prices and profits as possible, restricting the supply is, at times, the way to achieve your end. But that doesn't make the practice right, it only proves the point—that the capitalist system is, by its very nature, inefficient and wasteful.

The greatest waste of capitalism is war.

The all-out production of goods which is not possible in capitalist economy in peacetime is achieved in wartime. Then, and then only, does capitalism solve the problem of full employment of men, materials, machinery, and money.

To what end? Sheer destruction. Destruction of the hopes and dreams and lives of millions of human beings; destruction of thousands of schools, hospitals, factories, railways, bridges, docks, mines, power plants; destruction of thousands of square miles of farm land and forests.

No one can count the agonies of the wounded, the sufferings of the maimed and the mutilated, the longing of the living for the dead. But we do know how much money war costs. We do know the amount of waste in terms of dollars and cents. The figure makes crystal clear that the greatest waste of capitalism is war.

The first World War cost 200 billion dollars. In 1935, the authors of *Rich Man, Poor Man* worked out a yardstick by which to measure that. Here it is: "It would be enough money to give a $3,000 house [in pre-inflation dollars] and a piece of ground to every family in the United States, and England, and Belgium, and France, and Austria, and Hungary, and Germany, and Italy.

"Or with that much money we could run all the hospitals in the United States for 200 years. We could pay all the expenses of our public schools for 80 years. Or again, if 2,150 workers were to labor for 40 years at an annual wage of $2,500 each, their combined earnings would pay the cost of the World War for just one day!"

World War II cost over five times as much.

Nowhere is the waste of the capitalist system better illustrated than in war.

## 10. CAPITALISM IS IRRATIONAL

The capitalist system is irrational.

It is based on the premise that the self-interest of the business man is sure to benefit the nation; that if only individuals are left free to make as much profit as they can, the whole of society must be better off; that the best way to get things done is to let capitalists make as large a profit as possible out of doing them and, as a certain by-product of the process, the needs of the people will be served.

This proposition is definitely not true—certainly not all the time. As monopoly replaces competition it becomes less and less true. The interest of the profit-seeker may or may not coincide with the interests of society. As a matter of fact, they frequently clash.

The capitalist system is irrational because instead of basing production on the needs of all, it bases production on the profits of the few.

The capitalist system is irrational because instead of using the common-sense method of tying production directly to needs, it uses an indirect method of tying production to profits in the vague hope that needs will somehow be met.

It is as illogical and absurd as going from New York to Chicago, roundabout by way of New Orleans, instead of by the direct route.

Furthermore, a neat question concerning democracy is raised by the power of a handful of profit-seeking industrialists to decide, completely on their own, and in their own interest, whether or not the nation's needs are to be satisfied and at what price. It is not unfair to suggest that where the people do not control the economy in their own interest, economic democracy is supplanted by economic dictatorship.

This economic dictatorship, so dangerous to the welfare of the country in time of peace, can become a threat to its very existence in time of war. Regardless of the gravity of the crisis, the economic dictators insist that profits come before duty—and they are in a position to make the country pay their price. This is not an unfounded charge; it is confirmed by the experience of the United States in both World War I and World War II. A TNEC report, published in 1941, tells the story:

> Speaking bluntly, the Government and the public are "over a barrel" when it comes to dealing with business in time of war or other crisis. Business refuses to work, except on terms which it dictates. It controls the natural resources, the liquid assets, the strategic position in the country's economic structure, and its technical equipment and knowledge of processes.

The experience of the World War [I], now apparently being repeated, indicates that business will use this control only if it is "paid properly." In effect, this is blackmail, not too fully disguised. . . . It is in such a situation that the question arises: What price patriotism?"

The same irrationality in the system is exhibited when it allows business interests to let their greed for gain stand in the way of the conquest of nature for the service of the people. Almost every spring the Ohio river overflows its banks killing scores of people and destroying millions of dollars worth of property. Farm crops are ruined, homes uprooted and smashed, and cities inundated. This need not happen. The mighty river can be tamed, its wild energy can be harnessed, its seasonal fluctuations can be leveled off to provide a safe system of all-year-round navigation, and the soil, where it is wholly or partially destroyed through erosion, can be saved.

We have the know-how. It can be done. It has been done—in TVA.

Why, then, isn't it done? Why isn't TVA, America's highly successful experiment in regional planning, duplicated with an OVA—Ohio Valley Authority? And an MVA—Missouri Valley Authority?

Why? Because the capitalist system is irrational. The turbulent river must continue to go on its annual rampage leaving death and destruction in its wake because the flood control, power development, navigation system, the soil conservation, which an OVA could accomplish for the benefit of the many, would cut into the profits of the public utility companies, coal companies, and railroads. These business interests fought the development of power production and cheap water transportation in TVA and they continue to fight it in other river valley regions. Another proof of the absurdity of the basic premise of capitalism, that private interest and public welfare necessarily coincide.

Nowhere is the irrationality of the capitalist system more evident than in its lack of plan. Within each business there is system, organization, planning; but in the relationship of one business to another there is no system, no organization, no planning—only anarchy.

The economic welfare of the nation can best be achieved, industialists assure us, not by careful comprehensive planning to that end, but by allowing individual capitalists to decide what is best for themselves and hoping that the sum of all those individual decisions will add up to the good of the community.

It just doesn't make sense.

The capitalist system is irrational, also, in its division of the people into warring classes. Instead of "one nation, indivisible, with liberty and justice for all," capitalism, by its very nature, creates two nations, divisible, with liberty and justice for one class and not for the other. Instead of a unified community, with people living together in brotherhood and friendship, the capitalist system makes for a disunited community with the class that works and the class that owns necessarily fighting each other for a larger share of the national income.

The income of the owning class, profits, is looked upon as a good thing since the purpose of industry is profit-making; the income of the working class, wages, is looked upon as a bad thing since it cuts into profits. Regardless of the lip service paid to the merit of the "theory of high wages," that is the nub of the matter. Profits are regarded as a positive good to be made as large as possible; wages are regarded as a positive evil to be kept down to a minimum so costs of production will be low.

The resultant inability of the workers to buy back the goods they produce leads to crisis and depression—the periodic breakdown of the system. Could any economic system be more illogical?

Another irrationality that grows out of this emphasis on profit-making as the primary motive for the development of industry, is the confusion it creates in the values men live by.

What is the guide to conduct in capitalist society? That depends.

In the business world, competition, non-Christian self-interest, sharp dealing, cut the other fellow's throat, push your rival to the wall, anything goes that you can get away with; never mind what you will do with it, spend all your time and energy in the feverish pursuit of wealth—the bigger your pile, the more successful you are, regardless of how you acquired it.

In the world of family and friends, in the world of religion, other standards prevail. Instead of competition, cooperation; instead of hate, love; instead of grab for yourself, service to others; instead of climb to the top on the other fellow's back, help your fellow-man; instead of "how much is there in it for me?", "will it benefit others?"; instead of the lust for riches, the desire to serve.

Two sets of values—as different as night and day.

## 11. CAPITALISM IS UNJUST

The capitalist system is unjust.

It must be unjust because its foundation stone is one of inequality.

The good things of life flow in a never-ending stream to a small, privileged, rich class; while frightening insecurity, degrading poverty, and inequality of opportunity are the lot of the large, unprivileged, poor class.

This is one result of the private ownership of the means of production—the basis of the capitalist system. Another important result is the inequality of personal freedom between those who own and those who do not own the means of production.

The worker, in theory, is a "free" person who can do as he pleases. In fact, however, his freedom is severely limited. He is free only to accept the oppressive terms offered by the employer—or starve.

As President Roosevelt put it in his message to Congress on January 11, 1944, "Necessitous men are not free men."

The structure of the capitalist system is such that the majority of the people must always be "necessitous men" and therefore not free. They own nothing but their two hands; they must eat today what they earned yesterday; at 40, they are considered "too old" to work in mass-production industry; and always there is the overhanging dread of losing their job.

Another injustice of the capitalist system is the toleration of a parasitic class which, far from being ashamed of living without working, actually takes pride in it. The apologists for the capitalist system argue that though these parasites are idle, their money is not—the tribute they exact from those who work is the reward of the "risk" they take. To some extent, that is true—there is indeed a possibility that their money will be lost.

But while they risk their money, the workers risk their lives. Just how great are the risks the workers take? The figures are astounding. "Loss of life and injuries within our industrial plants during the war period far exceeded the casualties on the battle fronts."

In 1946, every 30 minutes, for 24 hours around the clock, seven days a week, an American worker was killed on the job by accident.

Every 17½ seconds, an American worker was injured.

Who really takes the risks in industry?

And what is the reward the workers get for the risks they take?

Here is a specific example, typical of capitalist industry:

In 1946, the union of shipyard workers in the Bethlehem Steel Company fought for and won an increase of 15 per cent which raised the minimum shipyard rate to $1.04 an hour.

That's $41.60 a week, or $2163.20 a year.

In 1946, the executives in Bethlehem were given a 46 per cent salary boost. Mr. J. M. Larkin, vice-president of Bethlehem, who insisted that the incentive rates for workers had to be cut, was given a bonus of $38,764 in addition to his salary of $138,416.

That's $177,180 a year, $3,407.30 a week, $85.18 an hour.

Mr. Larkin received *each week* more than one and one-half times as much as workers getting the minimum rate at Bethlehem received *in a year*.

Mr. Larkin received *every hour*, more than twice as much as the workers earned *in a week*.

Mr. Larkin's income, however large it may be relative to that of the workers, has the merit of being earned. He has performed a necessary function, and therefore has a legitimate moral claim to what he receives. But what moral claim to ownership does the man have who inherits a fortune and never does a stroke of work in his life?

Let us be clear about the significance of the institution of inheritance in the capitalist system. When a man inherits a million dollars it isn't just a pile of money on which he draws until nothing is left. It's not like that at all.

The million dollars is most commonly in the form of stocks or bonds in industrial or banking corporations. Some shares may pay dividends of 8%, some 2% etc. Let us assume that he has an average return of 4%. This means that by the simple fact of owning those shares, he has an annual income of $40,000.

Of all the wealth that is produced in the country every year, $40,000 worth flows into his pockets. He spends the $40,000 this year, and next year, and the year after. After 20 years he dies, and his son inherits the fortune. The son then has $40,000 a year to spend. And his son after him. And so on. And after generations of spending $40,000 every year, the million dollars is still intact! Who says you can't eat your cake and have it too?

Neither the man, nor his son, nor his son's son have ever had to soil their hands with work. Their ownership of the means of production has enabled them to be parasites living off the work of others.

Another crying injustice in the capitalist system is inequality of opportunity.

A baby is born into the home of a worker earning $2,000 a year at the same time that one is born into the home of the millionaire. Do they enjoy the same rights and opportunities? Will the food, clothing, and shelter of the one be as good as that of the other? Will the medical care, recreation, and schooling be similar?

It's no good to answer that "America is the land of opportunity," and the worker's son, if he has ability, can rise to the top. Ability counts for a great deal, but birth, social position, and wealth count for more. This does not mean that with ability, energy, and luck it is not possible for a poor boy to become rich. It is. But the chances for the poor, *as a class*, to rise above their station were always slim and are getting increasingly less possible.

Where opportunity is lacking, it is not enough to have ability. And opportunity is lacking.

That's what Supreme Court Justice Jackson told the members of the American Political Science Association some years ago: "The real curse of our system of private enterprise today is that it has destroyed enterprise, it does not offer an opportunity for enough of the ablest men to rise to the top . . . the dream of ability rising to the top is seldom true. . . . Parents labor and save to provide formal education for their children and when that education is finished there is no place for the boy or girl to go except to start at the bottom of an impossibly long ladder of a few great corporations dominated by America's sixty families."

On the state of education in the country, President Johnson said in 1965:

> How many young lives have been wasted; how many entire families now live in misery; how much talent has this great powerful nation lost because America has failed to give all of our children a chance to learn. . . .
>
> Last year almost one out of every three of all draftees were rejected by the armed services because they could not read or write at the eighth grade level. . . . Today as I speak . . . nearly 54 million have not finished high school. This is a shocking waste of human resources.

Inequality of opportunity in education extends even further. The President's Commission on Higher Education reported, in 1947: "One of the gravest charges to which American society is subject is that of failing to provide a reasonable equality of educational opportunity for its youth. For the great majority of our boys and girls, the kind and amount of education they may hope to attain depends, not on their own abilities, but on the family or community into which they happened to be born or, worse still, on the color of their skin or the religion of their parents."

The "color of their skin" means Negroes, and the inferior quality of education afforded to blacks is shown by a multitude of statistics. Here are two very significant facts from a 1967 report by the Bureau of the Census and Bureau of Labor Statistics entitled *Social and Economic Conditions of Negroes in the United States:* "The average Negro youngster in the final year of high school is performing at a ninth-grade level. . . . By 1963, about 7 per cent of all Negroes 25 to 34 years old had completed college compared to about 14 per cent of all whites in this age group."

If you have a black skin not only will your education be poorer, but you are more apt to die at birth, your illness is more likely to be fatal, your life expectancy will be shorter, the house you live in will be inferior, your chance of getting and holding a job will be slimmer, and your income will be lower. In 1966 the median income of black families—the colonial people within our own borders—was only 60 per cent that of white families.

In a system where the primary motive for the production of goods is the making of a profit, it is inevitable that profit should be regarded as all-important—more important even than lives. And so it is. In capitalist society, it is not uncommon for dollars to be valued higher than human beings.

The bodies of 111 men who died in the Centralia mine explosion on March 25, 1947 are grim witnesses to that truth.

These 111 men need not have died.

The operators knew the mine was unsafe because both state and federal mine inspectors wrote report after report telling them so.

Dwight Green, Governor of the State of Illinois, knew the mine was unsafe.

He knew because on March 9, 1946, he received a letter from the officers of the United Mine Workers Local Union No. 52, who wrote at the request of the men in the mine: ". . . Governor Green this is a plea to you, to please save our lives, to please make the department of mines and minerals enforce the laws at the No. 5 mine of the Centralia Coal Co. . . . before we have a dust explosion at this mine like just happened in Kentucky and West Virginia. . . ."

One year later, three of the four men who signed that letter were dead—killed in the explosion they had begged the Governor to save them from.

A state investigating committee—after the explosion—asked William H. Brown, supervisor of the mine, why the operators had not installed a sprinkling system.

He answered, "We honestly did not think it was economical for our mine."

"You mean you didn't want to bear the expense?" asked the Committee.

"That's right," Brown replied.

Dollars vs. lives—and dollars won.

## 12. CAPITALISM IS ON THE WAY OUT

The capitalist system is not only inefficient and wasteful, irrational, and unjust; it has broken down.

In a period of crisis the system collapses to such an extent that instead of society being fed and clothed and sheltered by the workers within it, society must assume the burden of feeding, clothing, and sheltering the jobless with systems of doles, home relief, make-work jobs, and the like.

Were it only in periods of crisis that the system checked production, then it could be argued that capitalism impeded the development of productive forces only temporarily, not permanently. But that is not the case. Professor Schlicter of the Harvard Graduate School of Business Administration says: "It is not, however, merely in times of depression that industry fails to produce to capacity. Under existing economic arrangements, most enterprises must *normally* restrict output in order to maintain solvency."

In spite of the enormous toll of human life and the huge economic losses which war brings in its wake, capitalist nations, nevertheless, continue their drive towards war; the stability of the system is thus endangered, the possibility of the annihilation of the human race is real, yet capitalism is no sooner finished with one war than it prepares for the next.

It has no alternative. The contradictions which beset it cause it to disuse or underuse its productive capacity in peace time. Only in war or preparation for war can it produce abundance. *It cannot live except by preparing the weapons for its own death.*

Capitalism is ripe for change.

The new system cannot be "made to order." It will have to grow out of the old system just as capitalism itself grew out of feudalism. Within the development of capitalist society itself we must look for the germs of the new social system.

We have not far to look. Capitalism has transformed production from an individual into a collective process. In the old days, goods were turned out by individual craftsmen working with their own tools in their own shops; today, products are made by thousands of laborers working together on intricate machines in giant factories.

Increasingly the process becomes more and more social, with more and more people linked together in larger and larger factories.

In capitalist society, things are cooperatively operated and cooperatively made, but they are not cooperatively owned by those who made them. Those who use the machinery do not own it, and those who own it do not use it.

Therein lies the fundamental contradiction in capitalist society—the fact that while production is social, the result of collective effort and labor, appropriation is private, individual. The products, produced socially, are appropriated not by the producers, but by the owners of the mean of production, the capitalists.

The remedy is plain—to couple with the socialization of production the social ownership of the means of production. The way to resolve the conflict between social production and private appropriation is to carry the development of the capitalist process of social production to its logical conclusion—social ownership.

Most business in the United States today is carried on by corporations in which the owners hold shares and get the profits, but the work of managing the enterprise is performed by hired executives. By and large the owners of corporations have little or nothing to do with management and operation. Ownership, once functional, is now parasitic. The capitalists, as a class, are no longer needed. If they were transported to the moon, production need not stop even for a minute.

Private ownership of the means of production and the profit motive are doomed. Capitalism has outlived its usefulness.

In its place a new social order is arising—socialism.

# PART III ... ADVOCATES OF CHANGE

## 13. THE UTOPIAN SOCIALISTS

Socialism is a system in which, in contrast to capitalism, there is common ownership of the means of production instead of private; planned production for use instead of anarchic production for profit.

The idea of socialism is not new. The capitalist system had hardly gotten into its stride with the coming of the Industrial Revolution and the growth of the factory system, when already its inefficiency, waste, irrationality, and injustice were apparent to thinking people.

Beginning about the year 1800, in both England and France, the evils of capitalism were brought before the public in pamphlets, books, and speeches. There had been such critics before—as early as the 16th Century and every century thereafter. But the earlier writers were, in the main, isolated thinkers who had never built up a following. Now that was changed. Robert Owen in England, and Charles Fourier and Comte Henri de Saint-Simon in France, may properly be termed pioneer socialists because around each of them developed a movement of considerable size. Their books were widely read, their speeches drew large audiences, and through them the idea of socialism was spread to other lands—including such far-off places as the United States.

They were not content merely with denunciation of Society As It Is. They went further. Each of them, in his own fashion, spent considerable time and effort on carefully considered plans for Society As It Should Be.

Each of them worked out, in the minutest detail, his own vision of the ideal society of the future. Though their private utopias were quite unlike and different in specific particulars, they were based on a common pattern.

The most important first principle in each of their utopian schemes was the abolition of capitalism. In the capitalist system they saw only evil. It was wasteful, unjust, without a plan. They wanted a planned society which would be efficient and just. Under capitalism the few who did not work lived in comfort and luxury through their ownership of the means of production. The Utopians saw in the common ownership of the means of production the production of the means to the good life. So in their visionary societies they planned that the many who did the work would live in comfort and luxury through their ownership of the means of production.

This was socialism—and this was the dream of the Utopians.

It remained a dream for the Utopians because though they knew *where* they wanted to go, they had only the foggiest notion on *how to get there*. They believed that all that was necessary was to formulate their plan for an ideal society, interest the powerful or the rich (or both) in the truth and beauty of their new order, experiment with it on a small scale, and then rely on the sweet reasonableness of people to bring it into being.

The naïveté of the Utopians is shown in the fact that the very groups they were appealing to were precisely the ones whose interest lay in keeping things as they were, not in change. They showed the same misunderstanding of the forces at work in society in their repudiation of political and economic agitation by the working class; in their insistence that only through good will and understanding by all men, not through the organization of workers as a class, would the new society be attained.

Equally unrealistic was their idea that they could succeed in setting up miniatiure social experiments in accordance with their utopian blueprints.

As might have been foreseen, their "islands of bliss in the gray sea of capitalist misery" were doomed to failure. The capitalist system could not be patched up in little isolated communities shut off from the rest of the world.

The Utopian Socialists were humanitarians who reacted strongly to the harsh environment of capitalism. They made valid and penetrating criticisms of the capitalist system and invented schemes for building a better world. While they were preaching their new Gospel, two men were born who were to approach the problem in a different way.

Their names were Karl Marx and Friedrich Engels.

## 14. KARL MARX AND FRIEDRICH ENGELS

The socialism of the Utopians was based on a humanitarian sense of injustice. The socialism of Marx and Engels was based on a study of the historical, economic, and social development of man.*

Karl Marx planned no utopia. He wrote practically nothing on how the Society of the Future would operate. He was tremendously interested in the Society of the Past, how it arose, developed, and decayed, until it became the Society of the Present; he was tremendously interested in the Society of the Present because he wanted to discover the forces in it which would make for further change to the Society of the Future.

Unlike the Utopians, Marx spent no time on the economic institutions of Tomorrow. He spent almost all of his time on a study of the economic institutions of Today.

Marx wanted to know what made the wheels go around in capitalist society. The title of his most important book, *Capital—A Critical Analysis of Capitalist Society*, shows where his interest and attention were centered. He was the first great social thinker to make a systematic, intelligent, critical analysis of capitalist production.

With the Utopians, socialism was a product of the imagination, an invention of this or that brilliant mind. Marx brought socialism down from the clouds; he showed that it was not merely a vague aspiration, but the next step in the historical development of the human race—the necessary and inevitable outcome of the evolution of capitalist society.

Marx transformed socialism from a utopia to a science. Instead of a visionary fantastic blueprint of a perfect social order, he substituted a down-to-earth theory of social progress; instead of appealing to the sympathy, goodwill, and intelligence of the upper

---

* Although we will refer continually to the ideas of Marx, the contribution of Engels to the development of socialist thought should not be minimized. Marx and Engels were in their twenties when they first met and they remained life-long friends and collaborators. Theirs was, without question, the greatest intellectual partnership the world has ever seen. Although Engels was a prominent thinker in his own right and had arrived at his basic philosophy independently of Marx, he was content to play "second fiddle" throughout their long association. In 1888, he summarized their relationship in these words: "I cannot deny that both before and during my 40 years collaboration with Marx I had a certain independent share in laying the foundations, and more particularly in elaborating the theory. But the greater part of its leading basic principles, particularly in the realm of economics and history, and above all its final clear formulation belongs to Marx. Marx stood higher, saw further, and took a wider and quicker view than all the rest of us. We others were at best talented. Marx was a genius."

class to change society, he relied on the working class to emancipate itself and become the architect of the new order.

The socialism of Marx—scientific socialism—was given its first significant expression a century ago with the publication, in February, 1848, of the *Communist Manifesto*, written jointly with Engels. This pamphlet, only 23 pages in the original edition, in which the essence of their doctrine is distilled, has since become the foundation stone of the socialist movement in every corner of the earth. It has been translated into more languages than any other book except the Bible; as the inspiration to the powerful worldwide working class movement, it is without question the most influential pamphlet ever written anywhere at any time.

In their intensive study of why human society is what it is, why it changes, and in what direction it is going, Marx and Engels found there was a connecting theme running through history. Things are not independent of each other; history merely *appears* to be a jumble of disordered facts and happenings, but in reality it is not a jumble; history is not chaotic—it conforms to a definite pattern of laws which can be discovered.

Karl Marx discovered those laws of development of human society. That was his great contribution to mankind.

The economics, politics, law, religion, education, of every civilization are tied together; each depends on the other and is what it is because of the others. Of all these forces the economic is the most important—the basic factor. The keystone of the arch is the relations which exist between men as producers. The way in which men live is determined by the way they make their living—by the mode of production prevailing within any given society at any given time.

The way men think is determined by the way they live. In the words of Marx: "The mode of production in material life dominates the general character of the social, political, and spiritual processes of life. It is not the consciousness of men that determines their existence, but on the contrary their social existence determines their consciousness."

Conceptions of right, of justice, of liberty, etc.—the set of ideas which each society has—are suited to the particular stage of economic development which that particular society has reached. Now what is it that brings about social and political revolution? Is it simply a change in men's ideas? No. For these ideas depend on a change that occurs first in economics—in the mode of production and exchange.

Man progresses in his conquest of Nature; new and better methods of producing and exchanging goods are discovered or invented. When these changes are fundamental and far-reaching, social conflicts arise. The relationships that grew up with the old method of production have become solidified; the old ways of living together have become fixed in law, in politics, in religion, in education. The class that is in power wants to retain its power—and comes into conflict with the class that is in harmony with the new mode of production. Revolution is the result.

This approach to history, according to the Marxists, makes it possible to understand an otherwise incomprehensible world. By looking at historical events from the point of view of class relationships resulting from the way men earn their living, what has been unintelligible becomes intelligible for the first time. Thus, the analysis in the Manifesto begins with this opening sentence: "The history of all hitherto existing society is the history of class struggles."

What part does the state play in the struggle between classes? The state is the creature of the ruling class. It is set up and maintained to preserve the existing system. Its role in capitalist society is explained in the Manifesto: "The executive of the modern State is but a committee for managing the common affairs of the whole bourgeoisie."

The first duty of the state in capitalist society is the defense of private property in the means of production which is the essence of the domination of the capitalist class over the working class. It follows, therefore, that if the aim of the working class is to abolish private property in the means of production, it must destroy the state of the ruling class and replace it with its own state. The working class can attain power—its revolution will be successful—only if the ruling class state is destroyed and a working class state is established in its place.

At first glance this seems to imply merely the substitution of the dictatorship of the working class for the dictatorship of the capitalist class. Is this the goal of working class revolution—to make the workers rulers over the class to which they had formerly been subject?

No. The dictatorship of the proletariat is only the necessary first step in the process of abolishing class rule forever—by putting an end to the conditions which make for division of society into classes. The socialist goal is not the substitution of one form of class rule for another, but the complete abolition of all classes; the socialist goal is a classless society in which every form of exploitation is eliminated. In the words of the Manifesto: "In place of the old bourgeois society, with its classes and class antagonisms, we shall have an association in which the free development of each is the condition for the free development of all."

Always and everywhere Marx emphasized the point that the transformation from the old class society to the new classless order will be achieved by the working class, the proletariat. He looked to the proletariat to be the active agent in bringing about socialism because it, the majority of the population, suffered most from the contradictions of capitalism, because there was no other way by which it could better itself.

Workers were forced by the horrible conditions under which they lived to band together, to organize, to form unions to fight for their own interests. Trade unions, however, did not spring up overnight. It took a long time for the feeling of unity of class interest to grow up, and until that happened, powerful organization on a national scale was impossible.

It was the expansion of capitalism with the Industrial Revolution and the factory system which enabled trade unionism to make tremendous strides. This had to happen because the Industrial Revolution brought with it the concentration of workers into cities, the improvements in transportation and communication so essential to a nation-wide organization, and the conditions which make a workers' movement so necessary. Thus working class organization grew with capitalist development, which produced the class, the class sentiment, and the physical means of cooperation and communication.

The proletariat, then, is born of capitalism, and grows with it. Finally, when capitalism breaks down, when it is beset with contradictions it cannot solve, when "society can no longer live under this bourgeoisie, in other words, its existence is no longer compatible with society"—when, in short, capitalism is ready for the grave, it is the proletariat which will bury it.

Marx was not an armchair revolutionist who was content with telling the other fellow what to do and why he should do it. No. He lived his philosophy. And insofar as his philosophy was not merely an explanation of the world, but also an instrument to change the world, he himself, as a sincere revolutionist, had to be not above the struggle, but a fighting part of it. He was.

In accordance with his belief that the instrument to abolish capitalism was the proletariat, he devoted whatever attention he could spare from his studies to the training and organization of the working class for its economic and political struggles. He was the most active and influential member of the International Workingmen's Association (the First International) established in London on September 28, 1864. Two months after it was founded, Marx wrote to Dr. Kugelmann, a German friend: "The Association, or rather its Committee, is important because the leaders of the London Trades Unions are in it. . . . The leaders of the Parisian workers are also connected with it."

Trade unions, which seemed to many people then, as now, merely organizations to improve the day to day life of the workers, had a deeper significance for Marx and Engels: "The organization of the working class as a class by means of the trade unions . . . is the real class organization of the proletariat in which it carries on its daily struggles with capital, in which it trains itself. . . ."

Trains itself for what? For the struggle for higher wages, shorter hours, better conditions? Yes, of course. But for the much more important struggle as well—the struggle for the complete emancipation of the working class, through the abolition of private property in the means of production.

Marx drove home this point in a speech to the General Council of the International in June, 1865. After showing that unless unions did carry on the day to day struggle, "they would be degraded to one level mass of broken-down wretches past salvation," he went on to explain that they must have a broader aim: "At the same time, and quite apart from the general servitude involved in the wages system, the working class ought not to exaggerate to themselves the ultimate working of these everyday struggles. They ought not to forget that they are fighting with effects, but not with the causes of those effects; that they are retarding the downward movement, but not changing its direction; that they are applying palliatives, not curing the malady. They ought, therefore, not to be exclusively absorbed in these unavoidable guerilla fights incessantly springing up from the never-ceasing encroachments of capital or changes of the market. They ought to understand that with all the miseries it imposes upon them, the present system simultaneously engenders the *material conditions* and the *social forms* necessary for an economic reconstruction of society. Instead of the *conservative* motive: '*A fair day's wages for a fair day's work!*' they ought to inscribe on their banner the revolutionary watchword: '*Abolition of the wages system!*'"

Always and everywhere Marx teaches his basic lesson—the only way out is a fundamental change in the economic, political, and social organization of society, with revolution by the working class as the means to achieve it.

Does this mean, as is generally supposed, that Marx was so much a believer in revolution that he wanted it anywhere at any time? Not at all. Marx was opposed to indiscriminate revolution. In the International he fought against those who called for revolution on principle, those who argued that revolution must be made because it should be made. The essence of Marx's thought is that the revolution, to be successful, must occur at the right moment; society cannot be transformed unless its economic development has made it ripe for change.

The basis for the change to socialism lies in the deep contradictions within capitalist society leading to its breakdown; in the creation, by the socialization of production, of the germs of the new order in the womb of the old; and in the increased class consciousness and organization of the working class, which takes the revolutionary action necessary to make the change.

Marx saw the capitalist system as part of the history of human development. It was neither permanent nor unchangeable. On the contrary, capitalism was an essentially transitory social system which, like every other form of human society, arose out of the system before, developed, would decay and be followed by still another system. For Marx, no human society was static—all were in a constant state of flux and change. His job, as he saw it, was to find out what produced the changes in capitalist society—to discover capitalism's "law of motion." He began by trying to explain it and ended not by apologizing for it, as other economists did, but rather by outlining a guide to action for the forces which would create a better society in the future.

Socialists believe that Marx's picture of capitalist society is sound, that it is closer to reality than the picture drawn by non-Marxist economists. On that point Professor Leontief of Harvard University, though he is himself not a Marxist, had this to say to the members of the American Economic Association several years ago: "If . . . one wants to learn what profits and wages and capitalist enterprises actually are, he can obtain in the three volumes of *Capital* more realistic and more relevant first-hand information than he could possibly hope to find in ten successive issues of the U. S. Census [or] a dozen textbooks on contemporary economic institutions. . . ."

In the same article, Professor Leontief paid tribute to the many predictions made by Marx which have since been fulfilled: "The record is indeed impressive: increasing concentration of wealth, rapid elimination of small and medium-sized enterprises, progressive limitation of competition, incessant technological progress accompanied by the ever-growing importance of fixed capital, and, last but not least, the undiminishing amplitude of recurrent business cycles—an unsurpassed series of prognostications fulfilled, against which modern economic theory with all its refinements has little to show indeed."

It is interesting to note that about the same time that this Harvard professor felt it necessary to suggest to his fellow economics teachers that they could learn much from Karl Marx, another distinguished scholar was offering similar advice to his colleagues in the field of history. In an article in the *American Historical Review* of October 1935, the late Charles Beard, one of America's most eminent historians, wrote: "It may be appropriate to remind those who may be inclined to treat Marx as a mere revolutionary or hot partisan that he was more than that. He was a doctor of philosophy from a German university, possessing the hallmark of the scholar. He was a student of Greek and Latin learning. He read, besides German, his native tongue, Greek, Latin, French, English, Italian, and Russian. He was widely read in contemporary history and economic thought. Hence, however much one may dislike Marx's personal views, one cannot deny to him wide and deep knowledge—and a fearless and sacrificial life. He not only interpreted history, as everyone does who writes any history, but he helped to make history. Possibly he may have known something."

The working class movement in almost every country of the world, striving to achieve social and economic justice, feels that he may have known something.

The colonial peoples of Asia and Africa, basing their struggles for liberation and independence on his teachings, think that he may have known something.

The countries of eastern Europe, attempting to replace anarchic production for profit with planned production for use, believe that he may have known something.

The privileged few in every capitalist country of the world trying desperately to remain secure on their tottering seats of power, tremble with the fear that he may have known something.

The people in a country one-sixth of the earth's surface, having successfully overthrown capitalism and demonstrated that socialism can end class division and enable man consciously to direct his economy for the welfare of all, are certain that he did know something.

# PART IV ... SOCIALISM

## 15. SOCIALIST PLANNED ECONOMY

We come now to an analysis of socialism. Let us be clear at the outset that believers in socialism do not argue that the change from private to public ownership of the means of production will solve all man's problems—it will not make angels out of devils, nor will it bring heaven on earth. The claim is made, however, that socialism will remedy the major evils of capitalism, abolish exploitation, poverty, insecurity, and war, and make for greater welfare and happiness of man.

Socialism does not mean piecemeal patchwork reform of capitalism. It means revolutionary change—the reconstruction of society along entirely different lines.

Instead of individual effort for individual profit, there will be collective effort for collective benefit.

Cloth will be made, not to make money, but to provide people with clothes—and so with all other goods.

The power of man over man will be diminished; the power of man over nature will be increased.

The capacity to produce abundance, instead of being strangled by consideration of profit-making, will be utilized to the utmost to provide plenty for all.

The overhanging fear of depression and unemployment, of destitution and insecurity, will vanish with the knowledge that planned production for use insures jobs for all, all the time—economic security from the cradle to the grave.

When success is no longer measured by the size of your pile but by the extent of your cooperation with your fellow man, then the rule of gold will be replaced by the golden rule.

Imperialist wars, which result from the profit-makers' hunt for foreign markets where they can sell "excess" goods and invest "excess" capital will come to an end—since there will no longer be "excess" goods or capital, and no profit-makers.

With the means of production no longer in private hands, society will no longer be divided into classes of employers and workers. One man will not be in a position to exploit another—A will not be able to profit from B's labor.

In short, the essence of socialism is that the country will no longer be owned by a few and mismanaged by them for their own benefit, it will be owned by the people and managed by the people for the benefit of the people.

So far we have dealt only with one part of that "essence" of socialism, the part about the country being "owned by the people" —another way of saying public ownership of the means of production. We come now to the second part of that definition—"managed by the people for the benefit of the people." How will that be accomplished?

The answer to that question is *centralized planning*. Just as public ownership of the means of production is an essential feature of socialism, so, too, is centralized planning.

Now obviously centralized planning for a whole nation is a tough job. It's so tough that many people in capitalist countries— particularly those who own the means of production and therefore think capitalism is the best of all possible worlds—are certain that it can't be done. The National Association of Manufacturers, for example, is emphatic on that point—it has repeated it again and again. Here is one of its plainest, most direct sentences on the subject from its "Platform for American Industry" some years ago: "No small group of men can possess the wisdom, foresight and discernment required to plan, direct, and stimulate successfully the activities of all the people."

Now this charge, if true, is extremely serious in any consideration of socialism. For socialist economy *must* be a planned economy, and if planning is impossible, then socialism is impossible.

Is centralized planning possible? In 1928 something happened which took the question of planning out of the realm of guesswork and brought it down to earth. In 1928, the Union of Soviet Socialist Republics set up its First Five-Year Plan. When that was completed, they started their Second Five-Year Plan, and after that, their Third Five-Year Plan (and so it will go, for ever and ever, so long as Russia is socialized—because, as we have seen, a socialist state *has* to have a plan.)

*Now* we need no longer guess whether or not it is possible for a nation to have centralized planning. Now we know. The Soviet Union has tried it. It works. It is possible.

Whatever anyone may think of this or that feature of Soviet life, regardless of whether he is a lover or a hater of the Soviet

Union, he will have to admit—since its bitterest enemies so admit—that it does have a planned economy. Therefore, to understand how a planned economy operates in a socialist country we must examine the Russian model.

What does a plan involve? When you or I make a plan, when anybody makes a plan, there are two parts to it—a *for* and a *how*, an aim and a method. The goal is one part of our plan and the way to get there is the other part.

So it is with socialist planning. It has an aim and a method. The late Sidney and Beatrice Webb (whose study of the Soviet Union, *Soviet Communism: A New Civilization?*, although published three decades ago, still stands as a magnificent monument to a lifetime of pioneer scholarship in the social sciences) show the essential difference between the aim of socialist planning and the ends sought in capitalist countries: "In a capitalist society, the purpose of even the largest enterprise is the pecuniary profit to be gained by its owners or shareholders. . . . In the U.S.S.R., with what is called the Dictatorship of the Proletariat, the end to be planned for is quite different. There are no owners or shareholders to be benefited, and there is no consideration of pecuniary profit. The sole object aimed at is the maximum safety and well-being, in the long run, of the entire community."

So much for the goal of planning in a socialist economy. We have already discussed the fact that the needs of the people, not profit, is the broad general aim. What we are chiefly concerned with here is not the *for*, but the *how*, not the aim but the method by which it is accomplished. What we want to know is what policies must be adopted to reach the desired goal.

Needs are limitless—but there is a limit to the productive resources which are available to meet those needs. The policies that are adopted must therefore be based, not on what Soviet planners would like to do, but on what it is possible to do. That possibility can be gauged only by getting a complete, accurate picture of the productive resources of the country.

That is the job of the State Planning Commission (Gosplan).

Its first task is to find out who and what and where and how about everything in the U.S.S.R. What are the natural resources of the country? How many available workers are there? How many factories, mines, mills, farms, and where are they located? What did they produce last year? What could they produce, given additional materials and workers? Are more railways and docks required? Where should they be located? What is available? What is needed?

SOCIALISM

Facts, Figures. Statistics. Mountains of them.

From every institution in the vast territory of the U.S.S.R., from every factory, farm, mill, mine, hospital, school, research institute, trade union, cooperative society, theater group; from all of these everywhere, from every faraway corner of this tremendous area, come the answers to the questions: What did you do last year? What are you doing this year? What do you hope to do next year? What help do you need? What help can you give? And a hundred others.

All this information pours into the offices of Gosplan, where it is assembled, organized, digested, by experts. "The whole staff of the U.S.S.R. Gosplan now amounts to something approaching a couple of thousand expert statisticians and scientific technicians of various kinds, with as many more clerical subordinates—certainly the best equipped as well as the most extensive permanent machine of statistical inquiry in the world."

When these experts have finished their job of sorting, arranging, and checking the collected data, they have their picture of Things As They Are. But that's only part of their job. They must now put their minds to the question of Things As They Might Be. At this point the planners must meet with the heads of the government. "The conclusions of the State Planning Commission and its projects were subject to endorsement by the Government, the planning function was separated from the function of leadership, and the latter was not subordinate to the former."

Planning, of course, does not do away with the necessity to make decisions of policy which the plan is to carry out. Policy is determined by the heads of the government, and the job of the planners is to work out the most efficient way of carrying out that policy on the basis of the material they have assembled. Out of the discussions between Gosplan and the leaders comes the first draft of The Plan.

But only the first draft. This is not yet The Plan. For in a socialist planned economy the plan of a Brain Trust by itself is not enough. It must be submitted to all the people. That is the next step. "The 'control figures' are submitted for perusal and comment to the various people's Commissariats and other central bodies dealing with the national economy, as, for instance, the Peoples' Commissariat of Heavy Industry, Light Industry, Commerce, Transport, Foreign Trade, etc. Each central authority refers the various parts of its Plan to the body next below it in authority, so that finally the appropriate part of the Plan comes down to the individual factory or farm. At every stage the 'control figures' are subject to a very thorough scrutiny and consideration. When they reach the last halt on the journey from the State Planning Committee, the factory or collective farm, all the keen workers and peasants take an active part in the discussion and consideration of the Plan, making proposals and suggestions. After this the 'control figures' are sent up along the same line until they finally return, in their amended or supplemented form, to the State Planning Committee."

Workers in the factory and peasants on the farm voicing their opinions on the merits and demerits of the Plan. This is a picture of which the Russians are justly proud. Often, it happens, these workers and peasants disagree with the control figures for their particular place of work. Often they submit a counterplan in which they give their own figures to show that they can increase the production expected of them. In this discussion and debate on the provisional Plan by millions of Soviet citizens everywhere, the Russians see real democracy. The plan of work to be done, of goals to be achieved, is not imposed from above. Workers and peasants have a voice in it. With what result? A competent observer gives this answer: "Wherever you go, at least in the parts of Russia which I saw, you will find workers saying proudly to you, 'This is *our* factory; this is *our* hospital; this is *our* rest-house'; not meaning that they, individually, own the particular object in question; but that it was functioning and producing . . . directly for their benefit, and that they were aware of it, and aware, moreover, that they were, at any rate in part, responsible for seeing that it was kept up to the mark."

The third stage in the preparation of the Plan is the final examination of the returned figures. Gosplan and the government heads go over the suggestions and amendments, make the necessary changes, and then the Plan is ready. In final form it is sent back to workers and peasants everywhere, and the whole nation bends all its energies to completing the task. Collective action for collective good becomes a reality.

Under socialism, through public ownership of the means of production and centralized planning, people can control their own destinies—man is master of economic forces. Production and consumption are based on a plan which asks: What have we got? What do we need? What can we do with what we've got to supply what we need? With such a plan it is possible to provide useful work for everybody who wants work and the right to a job can be guaranteed. Article 118 of the Constitution of the Soviet Union spells that out in these words: "Citizens of the U.S.S.R. have the right to work, that is, are guaranteed the right to employment and payment for their work in accordance with its quantity and quality.

SOCIALISM

"The right to work is ensured by the socialist organization of the national economy, the steady growth of the productive forces of Soviet society, the elimination of the possibility of economic crisis, and the abolition of unemployment."

The breakdown that came in 1929 is often referred to as a world crisis. It wasn't. The paralysis of production, with its accompanying unemployment and misery of the masses of people infected every part of the globe—but one. It washed against the borders of the Soviet Union—and receded.

The Russians were secure behind their dyke of a socialist planned economy.

Centralized planning is a characteristic feature of socialism. For an understanding of how planning works we have, of necessity, examined the Russian model—since Russia is, at the moment, the only socialist country in the world.

We should not, however, make the mistake of assuming that socialism in any other country must be exactly like that in the Soviet Union. It would not be. In a socialist United States, for example, there would be no need to hurry up the job of building industrial plant, since we already have the biggest and best in the world. Our first task, in contrast to that of the Soviet Union, would be to emphasize the production of consumers' goods.

So with other countries. Natural resources are different, climate is different, people's likes and dislikes are different, health, education, and culture are at different levels, concepts of freedom and civil liberties are different, history and tradition are different. The conditions peculiar to the Soviet Union, which led her to evolve the kind of socialism best suited to her needs, would not be the same in other countries, with the result that their socialism would be a different kind.

But the broad outlines would be the same for all countries which embrace socialism. In all there would be public ownership of the means of production and centralized planning.

## 16. QUESTIONS ABOUT SOCIALISM

*Can our economic system function without capitalists?*

Change the last word of this question and you will find it is a standard type that has been asked in every period of history. Four hundred years ago, in Europe, the question was: Can our economic system function without feudal lords? One hundred years ago, in the United States, the question was: Can our economic system function without slaveowners?

Just as society found that it could do without feudal lords and slaveowners, so it will find that it can do without capitalists.

A distinction must be made between capitalists and the means of production which they own as capital. Society cannot, of course, do without these means of production—the land, mines, raw materials, machines, and factories. These are essential. The difference is made plain by Robert Blatchford in his famous book, *Merrie England*:

> To say that we could not work without capital is as true as to say that we could not mow without a scythe. To say that we could not work without a capitalist is as false as to say that we could not mow a meadow unless all the scythes belonged to one man. Nay, it is as false as to say that we could not mow unless all the scythes belonged to one man and he took a third of the harvest as payment for the loan of them.

So long as the capitalist performed the necessary function of administration, so long as his income was earned, he was essential; now that he merely holds stocks and bonds from which he draws unearned income while hired executives do the work, he is not essential.

Ownership, once useful, is now parasitic. And who can deny that our economic system could operate—better than ever before—without parasites?

The fact of the matter is that we have reached the point where society not only can but *must* function without capitalists, since the power which is theirs as owners of the means of production must be used in such a way as to lead to unemployment, insecurity, and war.

### Will people work without the incentive of profit?

The best answer to this question is that most people work without the incentive of profit—right now—in capitalist society. Ask the worker in a steel plant, or a textile mill, or a coal mine, how much profit he receives for his labor, and he'll tell you, quite correctly, that he gets no profit at all—that profit goes to the owner of the plant, mill, or mine. Why, then, does the worker work?

If profit is not his incentive, what is? Most people, in capitalist society, work because they have to. If they didn't work, they couldn't eat. It's that simple. They work, not for profits, but for wages, in order to get the wherewithal to feed, clothe, and shelter themselves and their families.

There would be the same compulsion under socialism—people would work in order to earn a living.

Socialism offers additional incentives to work which capitalism cannot offer. For whose sake are the workers asked to exert themselves to increase output? Under socialism the appeal to work hard and well is based on the justifiable ground that it is society as a whole which benefits. Not so under capitalism. There the result of extra effort is not public benefit but private profit. One makes sense and the other doesn't; one inspires the worker to give as much of himself as possible, the other to give as little as he can get away with; one is a purpose that satisfies the soul and excites the imagination; the other is a purpose that entices only the simple-minded.

The objection is raised that while this may be true of the average worker for whom the incentive of profit has been largely illusory anyway, it does not hold for the man of genius, the inventor, or the capitalist entrepreneur for whom the incentive of profit has been real.

Is it true that it is the dream of riches which prompts scientists and inventors to work day and night to carry their experiments to a successful conclusion? There is little evidence to support that thesis. On the other hand there is ample evidence to support the argument that inventive genius seeks no other reward than the joy of discovery or the happiness that results from the full and free use of its creative powers.

Look at these names: Remington, Underwood, Corona, Sholes. You recognize three of them immediately as successful typewriter manufacturers. Who was the fourth, Mr. Christopher Sholes? He was the inventor of the typewriter. Did his brain child bring him the fortune it brought to Remington, Underwood, or Corona? It did not. He sold his rights to the Remingtons for $12,000.

Was profit Sholes' incentive? Not according to his biographer: "He seldom thought of money, and, in fact, said he did not like to make it because it was too much bother. For this reason he paid little attention to business matters."

Sholes was only one of thousands of inventors and scientists who are always so absorbed in their creative work that they "seldom thought of money." This is not to say that there aren't some for whom profit is the only incentive. That is to be expected in a gold-hungry society. But even in such a society, the roll of great names for whom service to mankind was the incentive is long enough to prove that scientific genius will work without the incentive of profit.

If ever there was any doubt about that, there can be none today. For the day of the individual scientist working on his own has long since gone. Increasingly, men of ability in the scientific world are being hired by the big corporations to work in their laboratories, at regular salaries. Security, a dream laboratory, the gratification that comes from absorbing work—with these they are content, and these they frequently have—but not profits.

Suppose they invent some new process. Do they get the profits that may result? No, they do not. Additional prestige, promotion, and a higher salary, maybe—but not profits.

A socialist society will know how to encourage and honor its inventors and scientists. It will give them both the monetary rewards and the veneration which is their due. And it will give them the one thing they treasure more than anything else—the opportunity to carry on their creative activity to the fullest extent.

Profit was indeed the incentive for the capitalist entrepreneur of long ago—but he has faded from the industrial scene. He has been supplanted by the new type of executive more suited to the change from competitive to monopoly industry. The recklessness, daring, and aggressiveness which characterized the old-style entrepreneur are not wanted in monopoly industry today. The big corporations have cut risk-taking to a minimum; their business is mechanized and planned; their decisions are no longer based on intuition but on statistical research.

These corporations are not run by the owner-entrepreneur of yesterday. They are not run by the owners at all—in the main they are managed by hired executives who work, not for profits, but for salaries.

Their salaries may be large or small, they may include a big bonus or no bonus. In addition there may be other rewards—praise, prestige, power, pleasure at doing a job well. But for most of the men who manage American business the incentive of profit has long since wilted away.

Will people work for other incentives than profit? No need to guess. We know that people do.

### Does everybody get the same pay in socialist society?

No, they do not. The skilled worker gets more than the unskilled; the manager gets more than the workman; the great musician gets more than the average musician; the farmer who produces 400 bushels of wheat gets more than the farmer who produces 300;

# SOCIALISM

the miner who digs eight tons of coal gets more than the miner who digs six; and so on. People are paid according to the quality and quantity of their work.

The person who receives even the largest income in socialist society can continue to receive it only so long as he continues to earn it through work. He cannot ever convert it into unearned income by buying the means of production and then living on the labor of others. He cannot buy the means of production for the excellent reason that in socialist society the means of production belong to the people and are not for sale. The higher pay he receives by dint of harder or better work enables him to live better than others who earn less; but his higher pay does not enable him to exploit anyone else.

Though there is inequality of pay in socialist society, there is equality of opportunity. Though skilled workers get higher pay, unskilled workers have ready access to the training and experience necessary to become skilled; though administrators, engineers, writers, artists get higher pay, free education for all in proportion to their ability to learn opens wide the entrance doors to these professions. And "all" in socialist society means exactly that—it does not mean all who can afford to pay the fees, or all whose manners are beyond reproach, or all who are not Negroes or Jews.

### What is the difference between socialism and communism?

Socialism and communism are alike in that both are systems of production for use based on public ownership of the means of production and centralized planning. Socialism grows directly out of capitalism; it is the first form of the new society. Communism is a further development or "higher stage" of socialism.

From each according to his ability, to each according to his *deeds* (socialism).

From each according to his ability, to each according to his *needs* (communism).

The socialist principle of distribution according to deeds—that is, for quality and quantity of work performed, is immediately possible and practical. On the other hand, the communist principle of distribution according to needs is not immediately possible and practical—it is an ultimate goal.

Obviously, before it can be achieved, production must reach undreamed of heights—to satisfy everyone's needs there must be the greatest of plenty of everything. In addition, there must have developed a change in the attitude of people toward work—instead of working because they *have* to, people will work because they *want* to, both out of a sense of responsibility to society and because work satisfies a felt need in their own lives.

Socialism is the first step in the process of developing the productive forces to achieve abundance and changing the mental and spiritual outlook of the people. It is the necessary transition stage from capitalism to communism.

It must not be assumed, from the distinction between socialism and communism, that the political parties all over the world which call themselves Socialist advocate socialism, while those which call themselves Communist advocate communism. That is not the case. Since the immediate successor to capitalism can only be socialism, the Communist parties, like the Socialist parties, have as their goal the establishment of socialism.

Are there, then, no differences between the Socialist and Communist parties? Yes, there are.

The Communists believe that as soon as the working class and its allies are in a position to do so they must make a basic change in the character of the state; they must replace capitalist dictatorship over the working class with workers' dictatorship over the capitalist class as the first step in the process by which the existence of capitalists as a class (but not as individuals) is ended and a classless society is eventually ushered in. Socialism cannot be built merely by taking over and using the old capitalist machinery of government; the workers must destroy the old and set up their own new state apparatus. The workers' state must give the old ruling class no opportunity to organize a counter-revolution; it must use its armed strength to crush capitalist resistance when it arises.

The Socialists, on the other hand, believe that it is possible to make the transition from capitalism to socialism without a basic change in the character of the state. They hold this view because they do not think of the capitalist state as essentially an institution for the dictatorship of the capitalist class, but rather as a perfectly good piece of machinery which can be used in the interest of whichever class gets command of it. No need, then, for the working class in power to smash the old capitalist state apparatus and set up its own—the march to socialism can be made step by step within the framework of the democratic forms of the capitalist state.

The attitude of both parties toward the Soviet Union grows directly out of their approach to this problem. Generally speaking, Communist parties praise the Soviet Union; Socialist parties denounce it in varying degrees. For the Communists, the Soviet Union merits the applause of all true believers in socialism because it has transformed the socialist dream into a reality; for the Socialists,

# SOCIALISM

the Soviet Union deserves only condemnation because it has not built socialism at all—at least not the socialism they dreamed of.

### Does socialism mean taking away people's private property?

Instead of wanting to take away people's private property, socialists want more people to have more private property than ever before.

There are two kinds of private property. There is property which is personal in nature, consumer's goods, used for private enjoyment. Then there is the kind of private property which is not personal in nature, property in the means of production. This kind of property is not used for private enjoyment, but to produce the consumer's goods which are.

Socialism does not mean taking away the first kind of private property, e.g. your suit of clothes; it does mean taking away the second kind of private property, e.g. your factory for making suits of clothes. It means taking away private property in the means of production from the few so that there will be much more private property in the means of consumption for the many. That part of the wealth which is produced by workers and taken from them in the form of profits would be theirs, under socialism, to buy more private property, more suits of clothes, more furniture, more food, more tickets to the movies.

More private property for use and enjoyment. No private property for oppression and exploitation. That's socialism.

### Aren't socialists preachers of class war?

Class war must exist so long as society is divided into classes with opposing interests. Capitalism, by its very nature, creates that division. Class war must end as soon as society is no longer divided into hostile classes. Socialism, by its very nature, creates a classless society.

Socialists don't "preach" class war—they describe the class war that already exists. They call upon the working class to help bring about the change from a society which must be divided into classes to a society where no such division is possible. They urge that universal brotherhood, which can be only a dream under capitalism, be transformed into a reality under socialism.

What the socialists preach is the gospel of Christianity, of human fellowship. That's what the *Encyclopedia Britannica* says about their teachings: "The ethics of Socialism are closely akin to the ethics of Christianity, if not identical with them."

### Aren't people in the United States better off than those in the Soviet Union, and doesn't that prove that capitalism is better than socialism?

Capitalism in the United States is over 150 years old, socialism in the Soviet Union is only 50 years old. To compare the two is, therefore, as unfair as comparing the strength of a grown man with that of a baby just beginning to walk.

Furthermore, the Soviet Union was a backward industrial country devastated by war and famine at its birth; it had just begun to grow when it was laid waste a second time in World War II. Obviously the relative merit of socialism and capitalism is not proven by choosing for comparison the richest capitalist country in the world, the one most advanced industrially and least affected by war's devastation.

A fairer comparison would be the capitalism of Tsarist Russia with the socialism of the Soviet Union. Here every impartial observer agrees that socialism is far and away superior in every respect.

Similarly, a fairer comparison would be that between capitalist United States and a socialist United States.

In no other country are the material conditions so ripe for socialism. Nowhere could the change-over from capitalist insecurity, want, and war, to socialist security, abundance, and peace be made so speedily and with such a minimum of chaos and discomfort. Where other countries on the road to socialism must make great sacrifices to obtain the industrial plant, scientific and technical knowledge, ours is ready to hand. In other countries, as in the Soviet Union, the people must go without, temporarily, in order to create the capacity to produce abundance; in the United States the productive forces have been built—they need only to be liberated. That, capitalism cannot do, and socialism could.

### Isn't socialism un-American?

For socialism to be un-American its aims must be not in accord with the spirit and tradition of the American people. Is that the case? What could be more American than the socialist goals of social justice, equality of opportunity, economic security, and peace —all American principles expounded in the Declaration of Independence and the Constitution? And have not these always been the professed ideals of our greatest statesmen?

The socialism of Karl Marx is a science. Like all other sciences it is universal and has affected directly or indirectly the thinking of millions in every corner of the globe—including America. But the test of whether an idea is American or un-American is not where it came from but whether it is applicable to America.

### Isn't socialism impossible because "you can't change human nature"?

The people who argue that "you can't change human nature" make the mistake of assuming that because man behaves in a certain way in capitalist society, therefore that's the nature of human beings, and no other behavior is possible. They see that in capitalist society man is acquisitive, his motive is one of selfish greed and of getting ahead by any means, fair or foul. They conclude therefrom, that this is "natural" behavior for all human beings and that it is impossible to establish a society based on anything except a competitive struggle for private profit.

The anthropologists say, however, that this is nonsense—and prove it by citing this, that, and the other society now in existence where man's behavior isn't anything like what it is under capitalism. And they are joined by the historians who say also that the argument is nonsense—and prove it by citing slave society and feudalism where man's behavior wasn't anything like what it is under capitalism.

It is probably true that all human beings are born with the instinct of self-preservation and reproduction. Their need for food, clothing, shelter, and sexual love is basic. That much, it may be admitted, is "human nature." But the way they go about satisfying these desires is not necessarily the way that is common in capitalist society—it depends, rather, on the way suited to the particular culture they are born into. If the basic needs of man can be satisfied only by knocking the other fellow down, then we can assume that human beings will knock each other down; but if the basic needs of man can be better satisfied by cooperation, then it is also safe to assume that human beings will cooperate.

Man's self-interest is expressed in his desire for more and better food, clothing, and shelter, in his passion for security. When he learns that these needs cannot be satisfied for all under capitalism as well as they can under socialism, he will make the change.

## 17. FREEDOM

Freedom, for most Americans, means the right to do and say what they please without interference by the state; and they take particular pride in their right to criticize the government and the people who run it.

These freedoms, of which Americans are so justly proud, are spelled out for them in the Bill of Rights, the first ten amendments to the Constitution. The guarantees are specific—freedom of speech, freedom from arbitrary arrest, freedom from imprisonment without a jury trial in all criminal prosecutions.

The importance of these freedoms cannot be overstated. They are precious liberties. They have been essential weapons in the struggle of the working class to better its conditions. They have helped make America great. Their existence here has assisted in building the nation by making the United States a magnet for immigrants from other lands. How long would Michael remain in the old country after receiving this letter from his brother Joseph rejoicing in his newly-found freedom? "Michael, this is a glorious country; you have liberty to do as you will. You can read what you wish, and write what you like, and talk as you have a mind to, and no one arrests you."

Americans have, without doubt, enjoyed these freedoms to a greater extent than have the people of most other countries. Nevertheless, it would be foolish to maintain that the rights guaranteed us in the Constitution always exist in fact. The freedoms which are ours on the books are not always ours in real life. Thus, the House Committee on Un-American Activities vilifies and persecutes citizens in utter disregard of the Bill of Rights. The rights of government employees to freedom of opinion and association are challenged in a presidential order outlining a new pattern of loyalty which departs from the traditional American concept. The Federal Bureau of Investigation is turned into a political police with endless files of secret dossiers on the beliefs and activities of millions of Americans. And the type of information which the FBI considers pertinent in its investigation of the new "loyalty" is indicated by this comment from an FBI report in 1948: "He is the kind of person who permits his Negro maid to come and go by the front door."

The facts tend to indicate that we can be too smug in our belief that fervid declarations of the freedoms we cherish and their reality are one and the same; nor are they made real by continued protestations of faith in them, or pious reiterations of our love for them.

Furthermore, freedom can be effectively denied or suppressed even when there is no direct coercion from the state. The examples are legion: Negroes in the South do not enjoy equal citizenship rights with whites, and everywhere in the country they are discriminated against in one form or another. Jews are plagued by restrictions which bar them from equal access to colleges, hotels, jobs. Screen writers are deprived of their livelihood because they insist on their constitutional right to keep their private beliefs to themselves. Commentators are driven off the air because they are too "liberal."

Is our proud boast of freedom to think and say what we please as substantial as we like to believe it is? Do we really tolerate all political and economic dissenting opinions? In ordinary times, it is true that we do not clap liberals or radicals in jail. But what happens in times of great tension, for example? And isn't it also true that jobs, power, and prestige almost always go to those who do not dissent, those who are "sound" and "safe"? Take the field of education as an example. We pride ourselves on academic freedom in our colleges. There are thousands of professors in the hundreds of colleges in the United States. By and large—in ordinary times again—they do have the freedom to teach what they think. But weren't they chosen in the first place because what they think is pretty much in line with what the heads of the colleges think? How many academically qualified socialists ever get appointments as teachers of economics on college faculties?

Freedom of the press is a noble, high-sounding phrase. It rings a bell in American ears. We like to think that it means the right of free public expression. Maybe it did once—but it doesn't anymore. The Commission on Freedom of the Press, headed by Dr. Robert Hutchins, formerly Chancellor of the University of Chicago, reported in 1947: *"Protection against government is now not enough to guarantee that a man who has something to say shall have a chance to say it.* The owners and managers of the press determine which persons, which facts, which version of the facts, and which ideas shall reach the public." [emphasis added]

We in America think that the whole question of freedom hinges on "protection against government"—on setting limits to the power of the law to dictate or control what we may say or do. But, as the Commission's report shows, the absence of restraint, by itself, is not enough—it does not "guarantee that a man who has something to say shall have a chance to say it."

The socialists argue that this is the heart of the whole question. For them, the absence of coercion, valuable as it undoubtedly is, does not necessarily insure freedom. The mere fact that no law prohibits you from doing something does not mean that you are in a position to do it. You have the right to go to the nearest airport and take a plane to New Orleans, or Hollywood, or New

York—but you are not really free to do so if you don't have the money to pay for the ticket. Of what use is it to have a right if you are not able to exercise it?

Freedom, then, means a lot more than mere absence of restraint. It has a positive aspect which, for the majority of the people, is of deeper significance. Freedom means living life to the fullest—the economic ability to satisfy the needs of the body in regard to adequate food, clothing, and shelter, plus effective opportunity to cultivate the mind, develop one's personality, and assert one's individuality.

This concept of freedom will probably come as a surprise to those who have always had the means to satisfy their desires and develop their faculties. *For them* freedom is measured solely in terms of non-interference with their rights; for the vast majority of mankind, however, freedom is measured less in terms of rights and more in terms of bread, leisure, security. We have only to ask a few questions to establish the validity of this broader concept: Is a jobless man who is starving, free? Is an illiterate, ignorant person, shut off from the world of books and culture, free? Is a man chained to a job 52 weeks a year with never a few days off for rest, vacation, and travel, free? Is a man continually beset with worries about making ends meet, free? Is a man in constant fear of losing his job, free? Is a talented person unable to afford the schooling which would help his talent flourish, free?

Only the rich are able to enjoy freedom in its broader sense of abundance, security, leisure. The poor are not free. Nor, as we have seen, can they win their freedom under capitalism. The struggle for socialism is, therefore, as Corliss Lamont aptly phrases it, a struggle to "share the freedom."

The road to freedom for the working class is clearly marked: to substitute collective for private ownership of the means of production—to establish socialism in place of capitalism. That way lies genuine freedom for the majority. As John Strachey puts it: "The initial act of dispossessing the capitalists creates at a stroke more liberty than has ever, or can ever, exist under capitalism, except for the capitalists. Neither constitutions, nor bills of rights, republics nor constitutional monarchies, can ever make men free so long as their livelihoods are at the mercy of a small class which holds sway over the means of life. In a socialist society alone those liberties, of which the workers of Britain and America possess little more than the shadow, can assume form and substance. In a socialist society the workers get, not merely the theoretical right, but also the practical daily opportunity to use their liberties. They are enabled to live, and not merely to work. Under socialism work

# SOCIALISM

becomes a means to a free and good life. Under capitalism the life of the worker is preserved as a necessary means to the extraction of the maximum possible amount of work from him."

While socialism is a condition of freedom for the mass of people, it deprives the capitalist class of the freedom it enjoyed. That's why we should greet the capitalists' outraged outcry that socialism and freedom are incompatible, with the question: Whose freedom? It is true that socialism is incompatible with the kind of freedom to which they have become accustomed. It abolishes their freedom to put their own welfare above the general welfare; it abolishes their freedom to exploit others; it abolishes their freedom to live without working.

But for the rest of us socialism would mean more, not less, effective freedom. And lest we worry too much about the capitalists' loss of freedom, let us remember that more freedom for those who have too little can only be won at the expense of those who have too much. In Abraham Lincoln's words: "We all declare for liberty; but in using the same word we do not all mean the same thing. With some the word liberty may mean for each to do as he pleases with himself, and the product of his labor; while with others the same word may mean for some men to do as they please with other men, and the product of other men's labor. Here are two, not only different, but incompatible things, called by the same name, liberty. And it follows that each of the things is, by the respective parties, called by two different and incompatible names—liberty and tyranny.

"The shepherd drives the wolf from the sheep's throat, for which the sheep thanks the shepherd as his liberator, while the wolf denounces him for the same act, as the destroyer of liberty. . . . Plainly the sheep and the wolf are not agreed upon the definition of the word liberty."

And just as plainly socialists and capitalists are not agreed upon the definition of the words liberty and freedom. For all the people to own the nation's means of production and manage them according to a centralized plan is freedom for socialists, while for capitalists it is the very opposite. Which is right? The socialist point of view has the merit, at least, of being consistent. If we are in favor of political democracy, as we certainly profess to be, then by the same reasoning, we should be in favor of economic democracy.

Capitalists no longer dare to argue against political democracy. But they do argue against economic democracy on the ground that it is a blow against freedom. Again we should ask the question: Whose freedom? Are they concerned for the freedom of all individuals to share in the joys of living, or are they concerned only for the freedom of private property in the means of production to keep its privileged position?

Freedom means living life to the fullest—the economic ability to satisfy the needs of the body in regard to adequate food, clothing, and shelter, plus effective opportunity to cultivate the mind, develop one's personality, and assert one's individuality. It is obvious that freedom in this sense is possible for all only when the greatest of abundance is attained.

The low level of human productivity which was the historical justification for the division of society into classes, for the exploitation of man by man, and for the enjoyment of freedom by a small minority only, no longer exists.

Now, for the first time in human history, it is possible to abolish classes, rid the world of exploitation, and enrich the quality of human life—by eliminating unemployment, providing the comfort of complete social security, giving general access to the world of culture, and making available time for leisure, study, and creative activity.

It won't be easy, it won't be quick, but with socialism, it can be done.

We are on the threshold of fulfillment of man's age-old dream of the emancipation of humanity—freedom for all, not for just a few.

## 18. THE ROAD TO POWER

Marxists hold that to transform society a revolution is necessary. They believe that the transition from capitalism to socialism cannot be achieved at any time, but only when the conditions are ripe for the transformation. They do not favor the seizure of power by a minority; the act of revolution can succeed only when there is relative social chaos, ruling class leadership is ineffectual, and a majority of the people supports the strongly organized class-conscious working class in its seizure of power.

Revolution is not merely a shift in the personnel of the government from one member of the ruling class to another, as the result of a rebellion or insurrection. For Marxists the term "revolution" has a much more profound meaning. It is the transference of economic and political power from one *class* to another *class*. The kind of revolution that Marx advocated, the socialist revolution, means specifically the transfer of power from the capitalist class to the working class; it means revising the relations between the working class and the capitalists so that the working class becomes the ruling class; it means the destruction of capitalism through the socialization of the means of production.

The seizure of political power by the working class is the first step in the revolution. The second step is to recast the social order and to crush the resistance of the capitalist class to the change.

Now because Marxists give the warning from historical experience that revolutions have been accompanied by the use of force and violence, it is popularly assumed that they "believe in force and violence." That is not true.

Marxists don't advocate the use of violence; no one in his right mind does. Marxists would like nothing better than to achieve their purpose of transforming society from capitalism to socialism by peaceful and democratic methods. They warn, however, that working class attempts to enforce the will of the majority for necessary change will be met by the resistance of the ruling class which will fight to the end to maintain the old social order; they insist, further, that the use of force and violence by the working class, once it is in power, is justified as a means of preventing its own overthrow by the counter-revolutionary use of force and violence by the dispossessed capitalists and their allies in other countries.

Marxists look upon the transition from capitalism to socialism as a translation from "despotism to liberty." They regard it as necessary and inevitable. They are well aware of the dangers. They expect that blood may be shed, lives may be lost. But, they ask, what is the alternative? Is the alternative to the loss of life that may accompany the socialist revolution, no suffering, no bloodshed, no violence, no loss of life? Not at all. The alternative is much greater suffering, more bloodshed, more violence, more loss of life—in capitalist wars. History books relate, with horror, the story of the thousands of people who were killed in the course of the French Revolution. It is, indeed, a tragic tale. But compare the total number of lives lost—estimated at 17,000—with the death toll in a single big battle of the last war. Compare the violence of revolution, 17,000 lives lost—with the violence of war, total military and civilian dead in World War II, estimated at 22,060,000, and the wounded at 34,400,000.

The alternative to the establishment of world-wide socialism with its inevitable accompaniment of peace is the retention of capitalism with its inevitable accompaniment of war.

The alternative to the construction of a new way of life is the possible destruction of all human life in the next capitalist holocaust.

A century ago, in the *Communist Manifesto*, Karl Marx and Friedrich Engels explained to the workers of the world why they must and how they could bring about the transition from capitalism to socialism, the next step in the historical development of the human race. On January 12, 1848, a few weeks before these scientists of revolution published their memorable work, a great American rose in the House of Representatives and said some things on a subject near to their hearts. Here is what Abraham Lincoln said on the right of the people to revolutionize: "Any people anywhere, being inclined and having the power, have the right to rise up and shake off the existing government, and form a new one that suits them better. This is a most valuable, a most sacred right—a right which we hope and believe is to liberate the world. Nor is this right confined to cases in which the whole people of an existing government may choose to exercise it. . . . A majority of any portion of such people may revolutionize, putting down a minority, intermingled with or near them, who may oppose this movement. Such minority was precisely the case of the Tories of our own revolution. It is a quality of revolutions not to go by old lines or old laws, but to break up both and make new ones."

### 19. HOW SOCIALISM WOULD AFFECT YOU

Socialism will not bring perfection. It will not create a paradise. It will not solve all the problems that face mankind.

It is only in artificially created, visionary systems of society, like those of the Utopian Socialists, that sinners become saints, heaven is brought to earth, and a solution is found for every problem. Marxist socialists have no such illusions. They know that socialism will solve only those problems which can be solved at this particular stage in the development of man. More than that they do not claim. But that much, they feel, will result in a vast improvement in our way of life.

The conscious planned development of the commonly owned productive forces will enable socialist society to attain a far higher level of production than was possible under capitalism. Socialism eliminates capitalist inefficiency and waste—particularly the waste of idle men, machinery, and money in needless depressions; it abolishes the even costlier waste of men and materials in capitalist

# SOCIALISM

wars, through the establishment of international peace; it accelerates the speed of technical progress; socialist science, unhampered by capitalist consideration of profit-making as the first and most important goal, makes tremendous strides forward. The standard of living for all is raised as increased production increases the quantity of goods available.

The entire change in the mode of life brings a change in the people who live that life. At first, man will carry with him into socialist society much the same outlook on life and work that he had in capitalist society. Steeped in the competitive atmosphere of capitalism he will not readily accustom himself to the cooperative spirit of socialism; soaked in the capitalist ideology of selfishness he will not quickly switch to the socialist principle of service to his fellow man. This unreadiness to change will even be true of many who have everything to gain from the change from capitalism to socialism; it will, of course, be particularly true of those former ruling class capitalists who lose their wealth and power in the transition from private to public ownership of the means of production.

But as the new socialist system of planned production for use takes root, changes take place in the attitude and development of the people. The capitalist taint in their mental and spiritual outlook fades away and they are reoriented in the spirit of socialism. The new generation, born and bred in the new society, becomes as used to the socialist way of life as the old generation formerly was to the capitalist.

The propagandists for capitalism would have us believe that socialism means the end of freedom. The truth is the exact opposite. Socialism is the beginning of freedom. Socialism is freedom from the evils which most sorely afflict mankind—freedom from wage slavery, poverty, social inequality, insecurity, race discrimination, war.

Socialism is an international movement. Its program in every country of the world is the same—to substitute for the barbaric competitive system, the civilized cooperative commonwealth; to establish the society of the brotherhood of man in which the welfare of each is realized in the welfare of all.

Socialism is not an impossible dream. It is the next step in the process of social evolution. Its time is now.

# MARXIAN SOCIALISM
## BY PAUL M. SWEEZY

Marxism is a body of ideas about the nature of the universe, of man, of society, and of history. It bears the name of Karl Marx, a German who was born in 1818 and died in 1883, and who lived the latter half of his life in London. Marx was a man of prodigious learning and enormously powerful intellect, one of the greatest thinkers not only of the nineteenth century but of all recorded history.

Marx combined in his system of ideas the realistic philosophy of the English and French Enlightenment, the comprehensive and dynamic point of view of the German idealists and particularly of Hegel, and the hardheaded analysis of the capitalist economy which we owe to the great British classical economists. The result was a brilliant new synthesis which is both highly original and at the same time stands squarely in the mainstream of modern intellectual development from the Renaissance onward. Here, in desperate brevity, are what I understand to be the central elements of the Marxian view of society and history:

The universe is real and existed for eons before there was human life, or for that matter life of any kind, on our planet. Life here on the earth is a natural by-product of the earth's cooling, and humanity is the result of a long process of evolution. In the earliest stages of society, human labor was still so unproductive that it yielded no surplus over and above the requirements of life and reproduction. As long as this was true, men lived in a state of primitive communism—cooperating, sharing, fighting, but not yet exploiting each other.

Later, techniques improved so much that a man could produce a surplus over and above what he needed for himself, and from this dates the beginning of economic exploitation and social classes. When one tribe fought and defeated another, it was now worthwhile to take captive the vanquished and force them to work for the victors. Some

---

*This is a slightly revised text of a speech delivered at the University of New Hampshire on May 22, 1956.*

men became rulers living off the surplus produced by others; while the actual producers lost their independence and spent their lives toiling for their masters. It was in this way that exploitation of man by man and the division of society into classes originated.

But the form of exploitation has not remained unchanged—indeed, nothing remains unchanged, everything is in a constant state of flux. The exploiters seek to expand the surplus at their disposal, and with this end in view they invent and introduce new and better techniques of production; the exploited seek to improve their condition and therefore carry on a never-ending struggle to enlarge their share of the product. As a result the forms of exploitation change, and with them the whole structure of society. At first it was slavery, in which the laborer is the property of his master. Next came serfdom, in which the laborer has attained a certain degree of freedom but is still tied to the soil. And finally there is wage labor, in which the laborer is legally entirely free but must work for the profit of others because he lacks means of production of his own.

A society based on private ownership of the means of production and wage labor is called capitalism. It came into the world first in England and certain parts of Western Europe, not all at once but gradually and painfully between the sixteenth and nineteenth centuries. It brought with it social and political upheavals, new ways of thinking, and a deep awareness of the vast creative potentials of human labor and industry. Historically speaking, capitalism was a long leap forward. In the words of the *Communist Manifesto*: "It has been the first to show what man's activity can bring about. It has accomplished wonders far surpassing Egyptian pyramids, Roman aqueducts, and Gothic cathedrals; it has conducted expeditions that put in the shade all former migrations and crusades."

But capitalism contains within itself what Marx called contradictions which prevent it from fully realizing the potentials which it was the first to uncover. The capitalist class, comprising those who own the instruments of production and set them in motion, is and must be concerned with making profits, not with the general welfare. Capitalists subordinate other aims to the maximization of profit. In pursuit of this objective, they pay workers as little as they can get away with and steadily introduce labor-saving machinery. The consequence, of course, is to hold down the consuming power of the working class. At the same time, the capitalists restrict their own consumption in the interests of accumulating more and more capital. But accumulating more and more capital means adding to society's productive capacity. We, therefore, have the paradox that capitalism steps on the brake as far as consumption is concerned and on the accelerator as far as production is concerned. This is its basic contradiction, and

# MARXIAN SOCIALISM

it cannot be eliminated except through changing the system from one of production for profit to one of production for use.

On the basis of this analysis, Marx believed that it was to the interest of the workers to organize themselves politically in order eventually to gain power and replace capitalism by a system based upon common ownership of the means of production and economic planning, a system to which he and his followers came in time to give the name of socialism. Moreover, Marx had no doubt that the workers would in fact follow this course, and that their growing numbers, importance, and discipline under capitalism would sooner or later ensure their victory. As to *how* the transition would be effected, Marx at first thought that it would have to be everywhere by means of a violent revolution. But as political democracy spread, especially in the English-speaking countries, he modified this view and in the last decades of his life believed that a peaceful and legal transition was quite possible in some countries and under some conditions. "We know," he said in a speech at Amsterdam in 1872, "that special regard must be paid to the institutions, customs, and traditions of various lands; and we do not deny that there are certain countries, such as the United States and England, in which the workers may hope to achieve their ends by peaceful means."

## What Is Socialism?

So much then for Marxism. Naturally, my account is oversimplified and very incomplete, but I hope it may serve to give you some idea of the scope and quality of Marx's thought—so different from the impressions which demagogic opponents have always sought to convey. Let us now ask: What is socialism?

Socialism, according to Marx, is the form of society which will succeed capitalism, just as capitalism is the form of society which succeeded feudalism.

The fundamental change would consist in the abolition of private ownership of the means of production. Please note that neither Marx nor (so far as I know) any other modern socialist of importance ever advocated or expected that private ownership of consumer goods would or should be abolished. On the contrary, he favored the multiplication of consumer goods in the hands of the lower-income groups, hence a great extension of private ownership in this sphere.

As to the form of ownership of the means of production which would characterize socialism, Marxists have never been dogmatic. Ownership must be by public bodies, but that does not necessarily mean only the central government: local governments, special public authorities of one sort or another, and cooperatives can also own means of production under socialism. And there can even be a certain amount of private ownership, provided it is confined to industries in which production takes place on a small scale.

A corollary of public ownership of the means of production is economic planning. The capitalist economy is governed by the market, that is to say, by private producers responding to price movements with a view to maximizing their own profits. It is through this mechanism that supply and demand are adjusted to each other and productive resources are allocated to various industries and branches of production. But public bodies have no compelling reason to maximize their profits (though, admittedly, under certain circumstances they may be *directed* to make as much profit as they can). In general, therefore, they must have some other principle to guide their economic conduct, and this can only be the following of a plan which coordinates the activities of all the public bodies.

Now socialists claim that it is precisely the freedom from the necessity to make profits and the coordination of all economic activities by a general plan which allows socialism to overcome the contradictions of capitalism and to develop its resources and technology for the greatest good of the people as a whole. Under such a system, crises and unemployment could only result from bad planning; and while bad planning is certainly not impossible, especially in the early stages of socialist society, there is no reason why planners should not learn to correct their mistakes and to reduce the resulting maladjustments and disproportions to smaller and smaller dimensions.

What about the non-economic aspects of socialism? Here Marx had a well-developed theory. He expected socialism to come first in the more advanced industrialized countries and to build on the political foundations which they had already achieved. Since in such countries the workers were in a majority, he believed that the taking of political power by the working class would mean full democracy and liberty for most of the people, though he also expected that there would be a period of greater or lesser duration when the rights and freedoms of the former exploiters would be subject to certain restrictions. As to the longer-run future, he reasoned that the full development of society's economic potential under socialism would gradually raise the well-being and education of everyone so that eventually all classes and class distinctions would be done away with. When that happened—but not before—the state as a repressive apparatus for dealing with class and other forms of social conflict would "wither away." The final goal of Marx and his followers can therefore be said to be the same as that of the philosophical anarchists. It would be a state of society in which, to quote Marx's words, "the free development of each is the condition for the free development of all" and in which distribution takes place according to the principle "from each according to his ability, to each according to his need."

Others before Marx had had a similar vision of a good society to come—a society of abundance and brotherhood in place of the society of scarcity and alienation which the human race had always been condemned to live in. What particularly distinguished Marx from his predecessors is that he purported to prove that this society of the future, which he called socialism, is not only a dream and a hope but is in fact the next stage of historical evolution. It would not come automatically, to be sure—not as the result of the blind decrees of fate. It would come rather as the result of the conscious, organized activity of working people, the vast majority of mankind. Given this perspective, the task of the humanitarian could only be to devote his energies to educating and organizing the working class to fulfill its historic mission. That, in a word, is what Marxists have been trying to do for nearly a hundred years now.

### Was Marx Right?

Marx's prophetic forecast of the end of capitalism and the opening of a new era in human history was given to the world in the *Communist Manifesto* in 1848. More than a century has passed since. Do the facts of this intervening period permit us to say whether Marx was right or wrong?

In the broadest sense, I do not see how it can be denied that Marx has been brilliantly vindicated. A mighty socialist movement based on the working class grew up during his lifetime. The crises of capitalism, far from abating, grew in intensity and violence, culminating in the holocausts of two world wars. Beginning with the Russian Revolution of 1917, more and more of the earth's population has withdrawn from the orbit of capitalism and has undertaken to reconstruct its economy and society on the basis of public ownership and planning. Today, something like a third of the human race has definitively abandoned private enterprise and, under Communist leadership, is building up a network of planned economies.

The fact is that over most of the world's surface the trend is now visibly away from private enterprise and toward public ownership of the means of production, away from market-dominated economies and toward economic planning. Only in the United States and a few countries closely allied to the United States does the trend seem to be in the other direction. Here, it is true, the socialist movement is at a low ebb, and private enterprise is very much in the saddle.

Should we perhaps conclude that Marx was right for the rest

of the world but wrong for the United States? Are we the great exception? Or are we merely lagging somewhat behind in a movement which eventually will be as universal as Marx predicted it would?

These are crucial questions, especially for us Americans. In what time remains to me, I shall attempt to indicate some possible answers.

There is one respect, and it is an important one, in which Marx was certainly wrong. As I noted earlier, he expected socialism to come first in the most advanced industrial countries. It did not. For reasons having to do with the late 19th- and early 20th-century development of relations between the advanced countries and the colonial and semi-colonial backward countries, the revolutionary movement grew more rapidly and had more opportunities in the backward than in the advanced regions. When the capitalist system was wracked by the destruction and disasters of the two world wars, it broke at its weakest points not at its strongest. Socialism came first to the Tsarist Empire, and spread from there to Eastern Europe and China.

This has, of course, meant that the early stages of the development of socialism have been very different from what Marx foresaw.

The new order could not build directly on the achievements of the old. It had no developed industrial base, no educated and trained labor force, no political democracy. It had to start from scratch and work under conditions of utmost difficulty.

Many people, including Marxists, expected socialism to proceed at once, or at any rate within a short time, to achieve its great goals: an economy of abundance, increasing democracy and freedom for the workers, a richer life for all. It could have happened that way if Britain, Germany, and the United States had been the first great socialist countries. But it could not possibly happen that way in backward Russia standing alone for a whole generation. The industrial base had to be built, and that meant belt-tightening. The Russians had no traditions of democracy and civil liberty, and under the difficult conditions of the '20s and '30s it was natural that a new police state should arise on the foundations of the old Tsarist police state. Moreover, like all police states this one committed excesses and horrors which had little if anything to do with the central tasks of construction the regime had set itself.

Under these circumstances, socialism in practice had little attraction for the people of the advanced countries. The standard of living of those living under it remained abysmally low, and political conduct, both among leaders and between leaders and people, often seemed closer to oriental despotism than to enlightened socialism. It was widely assumed in the West either that the Soviet Union was not socialist at all, or that socialism had been tried and failed.

In the underdeveloped countries, however, the USSR made a very different impression. They saw rapid economic advance, a vast process of popular education, some improvement in living standards—and never having experienced democracy themselves, they hardly noticed its absence in Russia. Communism was imposed on Eastern Europe by the Red Army chasing Hitler back to Berlin, but in China it was the product of a great popular revolution. And it is now expanding its influence throughout the underdeveloped regions of the world.

### The Competition of the Systems

The two systems of capitalism and socialism exist side by side in the world today. They are competing for the support and emulation of the backward and uncommitted countries. They are also competing in terms of absolute performance. How will this contest turn out? Will those now in the capitalist camp remain there? Or will they tend to join the socialist camp as time goes on? And finally, what about the United States, the leader of the capitalist camp?

These are questions which every serious person in the world is asking today. I predict that they will be increasingly the center of attention in the years and decades ahead.

The answers, I think, will depend very largely on the relative success of the two systems in the following fields: production and income, education, and liberty. I believe that socialism will win out in this great world-shaking contest, and I am going to conclude my talk by trying to give you some of the reasons why I hold this view. I should add perhaps that I don't expect you to agree with me at this stage of the game. The decisive forces and trends are still operating for the most part below the surface, and it will be some time yet before they can be seen and evaluated by all. But I hope that I may succeed in making you *think* seriously about these matters. It is, I believe, important that Americans should be put on notice that things are happening in the world, and will increasingly happen, which contradict their established thought patterns and expectations. You may not believe me yet, but at any rate if you pay serious attention to what I say you should not be surprised when things turn out differently from the way you have been taught to expect.

Let us first look at the relative performance of the two systems in the economic field proper. It will be generally agreed, I suppose, that United States capitalism has been doing about as well as can be expected in the last decade. Let us assume for the sake of the argument that it continues to do as well (though I myself think a good case can be made out for the view that this is too favorable an assumption for capitalism). Let us also assume that the USSR continues to grow at about its present rate, though I believe this is likely to be an under- rather than an over-estimate. On these assumptions, what will be the outcome of the economic competition between the systems?

The answer is clear and unambiguous. Here is the way the Oxford economist, Peter Wiles, put the matter in a broadcast over the BBC (I am quoting from the October 20, 1955, issue of *The Listener*, weekly publication of the BBC):

> Perhaps the most important fact in all modern economics is that the rate of growth of productivity is higher in the Soviet Union than in any important free country at the period of its maximum development, let alone now. That is, whether we take roughly comparable circumstances or the present circumstances, the Soviet superiority remains. The best performance by a large non-Communist economy for a long period together appears to be that of Japan: between 1912 and 1937 she grew by about 3 percent per annum. The Soviet economy grew by about $5\frac{1}{2}$ percent per annum before the war and by about $7\frac{1}{2}$ percent since 1948. For mining and manufacturing alone . . . the figures are: Japan 7 percent, USSR 12 percent.
>
> We see that the overwhelming Communist superiority in industry alone leads to a great overall superiority (in the whole national income). The effect of compound interest is very great over a few decades. Thus, growing 3 percent per annum faster than the United States, the USSR could catch up from a starting point of half the United States national income per head in 23 years.

These facts are not widely known in the United States, I am sorry to say, but there is no doubt about their authenticity. Thus, to give one example, *The New York Times* of May 18, 1956 quotes Mr. Hugh Gaitskell, leader of the British Labor Party and himself a trained economist, as having told the Convention of the International Ladies Garment Workers Union, meeting in Atlantic City, that "Soviet national income was going up 10 percent a year, double the United States rate." If this continues, the USSR will overtake and surpass the United States *in per capita income* in about four more Five Year Plans.

Let us turn now to our second field of competition, education. Developments here are no less startling, and unfortunately no better known, than in the field of economics proper. So far as the Soviet Union is concerned, I can do no better than quote from what former Senator William Benton of Connecticut wrote in the *New York Times*

Sunday magazine section on April 1, 1956, after a trip to the Soviet Union to study educational developments there:

> What is it that most impresses the foreign observer about the Soviet school system? In less than forty years, starting with a population about 50 percent illiterate, the Soviets have built a seven-year primary schools system rivalling our own in universality, with nearly 100 percent enrollment.
>
> Since World War II, the Soviet secondary school system has mushroomed amazingly. By 1960 the basic ten-year school is to be compulsory everywhere. In spite of acute labor shortages, all children are to be kept in school from 7 to 17. Every Russian youngster is to be given an education—a Communist education, of course, but comparable in its high standards of study and learning to an English public school or a French lycee. . . .
>
> Further, the USSR is on the road to surpassing the US both in the number and percentage of students enrolled in institutions above the secondary level. Indeed, when high level extension-correspondence students are included, the Soviet total of 4,300,000 enrolled in 1955 is already 70 percent over our 2,700,000. The Soviet Union offers as much training to every boy and girl as his or her talents and abilities will absorb. . . .
>
> Eighty to 90 percent of all students at Soviet higher institutions have been on state scholarships, which included stipends rising slightly from year to year. In February we learned from the Party Congress that beginning this autumn all education is to be free.

This speaks for itself, and all I would add is that the standards of the English public school and the French lycee are far above the average of our public schools.

The results of this enormous educational program are already beginning to show. According to Sir John Cockroft, head of Britain's Atomic Energy Establishment at Harwell, "Britain's output of graduate engineers was about 2,800 a year, while the figure for the United States was 23,000 and for the Soviet 53,000." (*New York Times,* April 14, 1956.) In other words, the USSR is already turning out more than twice as many engineers as the two most advanced capitalist countries combined. In science proper, Sir John estimated that the Soviet output was about ten times that of the British, and that the Russian scientists were fully as well trained as their British counterparts.

But maybe the capitalist countries are doing something to catch up in this all important field of education? If so, there are few enough signs of it. The secret of the Russian program, of course, is to train and vastly expand the number of teachers. To this end, teachers are treated with the greatest respect and are among the highest paid groups in Soviet society. The best graduates are enticed and urged into teaching: I have even heard from an American doctor who recently visited the Soviet Union that in medicine the top 3 to 5 percent of each graduating class is not permitted to practice but is, so to speak, drafted into the medical schools. How is it with us? How do we treat our teachers? What inducements do we offer to young men and women to enter the teaching profession?

Alas, I am afraid I hardly need speak of these matters to an audience like this. Whether faculty or students searching out what career to follow in life, you know all too well the answers to these questions. I will simply quote a few brief passages from a letter I happened to see in the *San Francisco Chronicle* (April 20) when I was recently in that beautiful city. It is signed by "A Math Professor, Ph.D.":

> . . . A teacher of science in the Soviet Union is reported to have an income in the very highest brackets, as compared with other occupations, whereas in the United States a teacher of science usually finds himself in the lowest income bracket; often he finds it impossible to maintain his family on a minimum living scale. . . . I have myself arrived at a certain eminence, with my Ph.D. in mathematics along with ten years of actual engineering experience besides 12 highly successful years as a professor. . . . Accordingly, I have been honored by the offer, which I have just accepted, to assume the position of chairman of the mathematics department of a leading private university on the West Coast. The job pays $5,500 a year. My son-in-law, who graduated from high school a few years ago and is now a bookkeeper, earns almost precisely the same amount. . . . Let us face the result: an economy which cares so little about its professors of science as to place them on a bottom rung is not entitled to ask for a leading world position in science, and we shall not achieve it.

It is a sad story, but all too easy to understand. There is no profit to be made out of education—not directly anyway. And it is profit that guides a capitalist society. As long as we have capitalism, we shall undoubtedly treat our teachers as second-class citizens, and educationally we shall fall farther and farther behind a society which puts science and education above dollars.

We come finally to the question of liberty. Here the advanced capitalist countries started with an advantage over the Soviet Union no less enormous than in the field of economics. And on the whole, they have succeeded in preserving their lead more successfully here than in economics. The Soviet police state certainly has an unenviable record of arbitrary arrests, trials, purges, shootings, labor camps, and all the rest—you are much more familiar with this than with the Soviet Union's record in production and education. The question for the future really is whether these are necessary features of socialism as such or whether they result from Russia's dark past, from the almost unimaginable difficulties of building an industrial economy in a backward country against implacable outside hostility, and from the tensions and fears of a world in which war is an ever-present threat.

There is no certain way of answering this question yet. I can only say that as a convinced socialist, I see no reason for despair and every reason for hope. I do not myself attribute much of the Soviet Union's record in the field of liberty to the evil doings of any one man, including Stalin. One-man interpretations of history are too easy—and really explain nothing. And yet there is no doubt that the last few years, which happen to be the years since Stalin's death, have witnessed a considerable change in the Soviet world, and the pace of this change has been sharply stepped up in recent months. Many of the abuses of the past were sharply denounced at the February Congress of the Communist Party. Since then, we have been told that a new judicial code is soon to be promulgated which will bring the USSR closer to our idea of a government of laws rather than of men. The labor camps have mostly been closed, and it has just been announced that they will soon be abolished altogether. Workers can now leave their jobs by simply giving two weeks notice. A friend of mine who is a professor at Stanford University happened to be in Moscow on his way to India in December and again in March on his way back. He reports that the whole atmosphere, and especially the attitude toward foreigners, had undergone a startling change for the better.

Is all this merely a temporary aberration, or is it the beginning of a new trend toward liberalization in the socialist countries? I myself firmly believe the latter to be the correct interpretation. And I think the cause is clear: the forced march in the economic sphere is drawing to a close; Soviet citizens now constitute one of the best educated publics in the world; the achievement of atomic parity with the United States has given them an unprecedented feeling of security; and the Soviet Union, far from being isolated, is now surrounded by friends and allies, including the most populous country in the world. The preconditions for internal relaxation and liberalization are there. What is especially encouraging to all who love liberty, and that certainly includes the vast majority of the world's socialists, is that relaxation and liberalization *are actually happening*.

I believe that the trend is here to stay, barring another war which I think increasingly less likely. In the long run, it will present capitalism with the greatest challenge of all. Up to now, the defenders of capitalism have always been able to counter arguments for socialism with the reply: "Look at the slave labor camps in Russia!" And there's no doubt that it has been an effective argument. Now, however, the camps are disappearing. Suppose all that they symbolize also disappears? Suppose socialism shows what Marxists have always maintained, that it is possible to have economic collectivism *and* freedom? Suppose the socialist world overtakes and surpasses the capitalist world not only in production and per capita income, not only in education and science, but also in freedom and respect for the dignity of the individual? What then?

You may think these questions fantastic now. Perhaps. But let me make a suggestion. Let me propose that you file them away in the back of your mind and then bring them out, say once every year, and check the answers you are able to give on the basis of the latest facts available to you. I have no doubt what the answers will be, sooner or later. If I am right, it will be facts and not my arguments that will convince you. And I am very glad to leave it to the future to decide.

# THE RESPONSIBILITY OF THE SOCIALIST
## BY LEO HUBERMAN

For socialists, history is not a jumble of disordered facts and happenings; it is not chaotic; it conforms to a definite pattern of laws of development. The economics, politics, law, religion, education, of every civilization are tied together; each depends on the other and is what it is because of the others. Of all these forces, the economic is the most important—the basic factor. The keystone of the arch is the relations which exist between men as producers. The way in which men live is determined by the way they make their living—by the mode of production prevailing within any given society at any given time.

The American economic system, capitalism, is a system of production in which the primary object is not the satisfaction of people's needs but the making of profit. It doesn't make any difference to a capitalist what he makes—so long as he makes money.

The capitalist system involves social relationships, the association in the process of production of two groups, employers and workers. The employers, relatively small in number, own the means of production—the land, forests, mines, factories, machines, and railroads. The workers, large in number, own only their capacity to work. It is from the association of these two groups that capitalist production ensues.

The means of production are operated for the profit of the capitalist class which owns them. When there is no prospect of a profit, then the wheels of industry stop turning, and men are idle, and machines are idle. And when that happens, neither patriotism nor concern for the welfare of society will serve to induce the capitalists to start the wheels of industry going again. The only thing

---

*This is the text, somewhat modified, of an address delivered at a meeting of the* Monthly Review Associates *on December* 15, 1950.

that will persuade them is the prospect of making a profit.

One class lives by owning; the other class lives by working.

The interests of the owners of the means of production, and of those who work for them in capitalist society, are necessarily opposed. It is to the interest of the capitalist class to preserve and extend its privilege and its power. It is to the interest of the working class to resist degradation and improve its social and economic position.

Between the two classes, in capitalist society, a struggle goes on —always.

Since the privilege and power of the capitalist are measured by how much money he has, it becomes his primary object in life to keep adding to his pile. In fact, he has no choice. To stay in business at all, to meet the competition of others and preserve what he has, the capitalist must keep constantly expanding his capital. The system *forces* the capitalist to seek more profits, so he can accumulate more capital, so he can make more profits. This is a never-ending process.

But there is another half to the economic shears. The capitalist has to pay as low wages as possible so he may continue the necessary policy of ever-increasing accumulation. However, the low wages which help make the high profits possible, spell a lack of purchasing power by the workers to absorb the output. People have need of, but can't pay for, the things that are produced.

The expansion of industry outstrips the expansion of purchasing power. This is an insoluble contradiction of which the inevitable result is those breakdowns of the system which we call depressions.

The socialist emphasizes that boom-and-bust is not a happen-so; it is not an accident; it is not due to a mistake made by stupid administrators of the country, by the Democrats or Republicans who happen to be in power. Boom-and-bust is inherent in the structure of the system; the capitalist system *must* work that way.

The basic problem of the capitalist system—what to do with its surplus of goods that can't be sold, and surplus of capital that can't be profitably invested, is solved temporarily, by imperialism and war —or by preparation for war through large-scale production of armaments.

The United States is not, as capitalist propagandists would have us believe, exempt from this process. It was not exempt in the 1930's when as many as one-fourth of all employable workers who were willing and wanted to work could not find jobs.

But wasn't the problem solved by the New Deal? Didn't NRA, AAA, WPA, and PWA put everybody back to work? They did not.

In spite of the billions of dollars spent on projects for relief and recovery by the Roosevelt administration, the army of the unemployed never fell below 8 million during his first two terms of office.

What took us out of that depression was World War II. And what is keeping us from falling back into another, possibly worse one, is the war in Korea and armament expenditure for World War III. This and nothing else is what is keeping the productive machine going full blast and our people at work. This is so obvious that even non-socialists admit it. On March 3, 1951, the Boston *Globe* quoted Thurman Arnold, former head of the Anti-trust Division of the Department of Justice: "Our production system has gotten ahead of our ability to distribute goods. The only way we can keep up with production is to wage war—a method of distributing goods when there's no other market."

I have sketched only the outlines of the socialist analysis of capitalism. There is more to the picture, of course.

There is the fact that the system is wasteful. It is wasteful because in its concern for increased price and profitability instead of for human needs, it sanctions the deliberate destruction of crops and goods.

It is wasteful because it does not always provide useful work for those who want to work—at the same time that it allows thousands of physically and mentally able persons to live without working.

It is wasteful because periodically all its men, materials, machinery, and money must be devoted to war, the merciless destroyer of all that is good in life, as well as of life itself.

The capitalist system is irrational. It is irrational *in its very nature,* in that, instead of basing production on the needs of all, it bases production on the profits of the few.

It is irrational in that it does not even aim to achieve the economic welfare of the nation by careful comprehensive planning to that end; but by allowing individual capitalists to decide what is best for themselves, and hoping that the sum of all those individual decisions will somehow, in some way, add up to the good of the community.

It is irrational in its division of the people into warring classes. Instead of a unified community with people living together in brotherhood and friendship, the capitalist system makes for a disunited community with the class that works and the class that owns necessarily fighting each other for a larger share of the national income.

It is irrational in the confusion it creates in the values men live by. This is well illustrated by F. P. A.'s poem:

## FOR THE OTHER 364 DAYS

Christmas is over. Uncork your ambition!
Back to the battle! Come on, competition!
Down with all sentiment, can scrupulosity!
Commerce has nothing to gain by jocosity;
Money is all that is worth all your labors;
Crowd your competitors, nix on your neighbors!
Push 'em aside in a passionate hurry,
Argue and bustle and bargain and worry!
Frenzy yourself into sickness and dizziness—
Christmas is over and business is business.

The capitalist system is unjust. Its foundation stone is inequality, with the good things of life flowing in a never-ending stream to a small, privileged, rich class; while frightening insecurity, degrading poverty, and inequality of opportunity are the lot of the large, unprivileged, poor class. This is true of the United States, the strongest, richest, capitalist nation on earth. I need cite only one figure of a report on the distribution of income published by a Congressional Committee in 1949: 25 percent of American families had a total income of $2000 a year—less than $40 a week. At the same time, government economists noted that over $3000 a year was needed for a satisfactory minimum standard—and nearly half the families in the country weren't getting it.

This topsy-turvy set-up in which waste and injustice, insecurity and want, unemployment and war, are inherent in the structure of the economic system, is maintained by the coercive agency of the state. "The state," in Marx's phrase, "is the executive committee of the ruling class"; in Woodrow Wilson's phrase: "The masters of the government of the United States are the combined capitalists and manufacturers of the United States."

Economic systems are born, develop to maturity, decay, then are supplanted by other economic systems. So it was with feudalism; so it will be with capitalism.

But the new system cannot be made to order. It must grow out of the conditions created by the old society. The socialist believes that within the development of capitalist society itself, there are the germs of the new social system which will supplant it.

He points to the fact that capitalism has transformed production from an individual to a collective process. The Temporary National Economic Committee of the United States Congress said in its *Final Report*: "No clear understanding of the modern economic problem is possible by anyone who does not first understand that the commercial and industrial life of the modern world is carried on, not by men in their individual capacities, but by men in their group or collective capacities."

That's true. But the product of this collective activity does not belong to those who have produced it. In capitalist society, things are cooperatively operated and cooperatively made, but they are not cooperatively owned by those who made them.

Therein lies the fundamental contradiction in capitalist society —the fact that while production is social, the result of collective effort and labor, appropriation is private, individual. The products, produced socially, are appropriated not by the producers, but by the owners of the means of production, the capitalists. And in most cases, those owners have little or nothing to do with production. Ownership, once functional, is now parasitic. The capitalists, as a class, are no longer needed. If they were transported to the moon, production need not stop even for a minute.

The remedy is plain—to couple with the socialization of production, the social ownership of the means of production. The way to resolve the conflict between social production and private appropriation is to carry the development of the capitalist process of social production to its logical conclusion—social ownership.

Social ownership of the means of production, instead of private; planned production for use instead of anarchic production for profit —that is the socialist's answer.

Socialism does not mean piecemeal, patchwork reform of capitalism. It means a revolutionary change—the reconstruction of society along entirely different lines. The principles and laws which govern a socialized and planned economy are completely unlike those which govern a capitalist economy.

In place of the *disorder* arising when each separate owner of the means of production does as he pleases, when he pleases, the socialist system substitutes *order*, through organized effort and plan.

Economic decisions are based not on how much profit can be made, but on what the people need. Cloth is made, not to make money, but to provide people with clothes—and so with all other goods.

The capacity to produce abundance, instead of being strangled by consideration of profit-making, is utilized to the utmost to provide plenty for all.

The overhanging fear of depression and unemployment vanishes with the knowledge that planned production for use insures jobs for all, with economic security from the cradle to the grave.

Imperialist wars, which result from the profit makers' hunt for foreign markets where they can sell "excess" goods, and invest "excess" capital, come to an end—since there are no longer excess goods or capital, and no profit-makers.

In short, the very structure of the socialist system is such as to eliminate those major evils which the very structure of the capitalist system creates.

This, in broad outline, is the socialist's analysis of capitalism and socialism. This is what he believes. And events since 1917 in the rest of the world, have reaffirmed his faith. For the socialist analysis has been confirmed. The prediction that the world will move toward socialism has come true. Socialism has already become the established way of life for some 200 million people. It is fast becoming the way of life for an additional 600 million people. These two groups together make up approximately one-third of the earth's population.

It is not surprising that this great forward march of socialism has alarmed the ruling class of our country. Alarmed it, in spite of the fact that the United States is the richest, most powerful stronghold of capitalism; in spite of the fact that internally, it is strong, its propaganda machine highly effective; and in spite of the fact that at the present moment, the working class is not in a position seriously to oppose it—the leaders of labor give only feeble resistance to its economic dictatorship at home and actually foster its expansionist and anti-socialist policy abroad. The ruling class has, today, no organized opposition of any consequence.

I need not dwell on the measures it has nevertheless taken to silence that opposition, on the anti-Left hysteria that pervades the country, on the Smith Act, the McCarran Act, the growing practice of punishing people, not for crimes they commit, but for opinions they hold.

The question we are discussing is what does a socialist do in such an America—in a country where the prevailing atmosphere is that of the witch-hunt?

I have no pat answer. I have no easy formula which will make everything simple. But this I do know. That if you believe that the solution to the problems that beset us is socialism, then it is your job to teach socialism whenever and wherever you can.

To the familiar argument that "the American people are not ready for socialism," I answer, "how and when will they be made ready, if socialism is not taught?" You cannot have a socialist movement without first having a socialist consciousness. The first and foremost responsibility of the serious socialist is to create a socialist consciousness, to make plain the socialist goal and the effective socialist means.

I do not forget that it is only through the activity of a mass working-class movement, which understands the roots of its exploitation and insecurity, that the change from capitalism to socialism can be effected. But it is only when the working class is armed with socialist knowledge that it can become the active creative organizer of those conditions which can put an end to capitalism.

There are periods in history when all emphasis must be laid on building such a mass movement. It is doubtful, however, whether in this country the successful achievement of that goal is possible today. The working class does not have a socialist consciousness; its leadership heads the wolf-pack in the hunt for radicals. Right now the best we can hope for is to keep alive a socialist *propaganda and education movement* against the day when the working class movement can hit its stride in the forward march to its socialist goal.

Right now, socialists will be accomplishing a great deal if they succeed merely in keeping alive the faith. For us, as for the early Christians, preaching our gospel is the supreme duty.

Because the times are difficult, we must learn to do our job more skillfully, more effectively than before. We must follow the prescription laid down by H. G. Wells in *This Misery of Boots*: "We have to think about socialism, read about it, discuss it; so that we may be assured and clear and persuasive about it." This we must do, whatever our walk of life; the soil is more ready than we think—we must plant the seeds from which a socialist consciousness can grow.

We must, of course, engage in the day-to-day struggles, the fight against the McCarran Act, the fight to get the soldiers out of Korea, the fight for peace. But make no mistake about it. You cannot win people to socialism simply by engaging in struggles for their everyday interests; it is *not* true, as is too often supposed, that marching on a picket line, or organizing a tenants' council, or working hard for the election of Progressive Party candidates automatically makes socialists out of those who participate. Nothing could be further from the truth. The everyday struggle is the best means available to reach people—but they will be made into *socialists* only if the moral is drawn plainly and clearly.

The immediate struggle is a vehicle toward the goal—but only if it is steered in that direction. If not, it is a vehicle which never reaches the goal but comes to a halt in a bog of reformism.

It is important to agitate for peace; but socialists must go a step further. They must make clear not only that our troops should be pulled out of Korea, but why, in the nature of the capitalist system, they were sent there in the first place. They must show how secure and lasting peace is attainable only through socialism.

In short, the job is to couple wisely the immediate with the ultimate objective. The day-to-day struggle is important of itself; but for socialists it is doubly important as a tool for teaching, as a means whereby socialist understanding can be achieved and socialist consciousness can be cultivated.

We are in a grim period of history, but it is not for socialists to despair. Despair is the prerogative of the ruling class—it is their world that is crumbling, not ours.

Socialists are the trustees of social rationality. We have a great responsibility. To bend all our efforts to the task of getting rid of the insane, destructive, capitalist system, and of replacing it with a system which permits rational intelligence to function—that is our job.

# AN ECONOMIC PROGRAM FOR AMERICA
## BY PAUL M. SWEEZY

I am going to plead a case which is unpopular in our country and probably will remain so for some time to come. Socialism is a bogey with which you frighten little children, and no one who wants to get ahead in the world can be suspected of having the least sympathy with it. But this is no excuse for ignorance, and I ask the reader's attention not because I expect to convince him but because I think he owes it to himself to learn the reasons and the arguments which could persuade at least one person to embrace the horrid doctrine. In addition, I think a look at history may convince him that socialism has more of a future, even in the United States, than its opponents would be willing to admit. Is it not true that the heterodoxies of today have ever been the orthodoxies of tomorrow?

### I

The American economic system is called capitalism. It is a system in which most of the means of production—the factories and farms, the mines and forests, the railroads and ships—are owned by a relatively few capitalists and operated for their profit. Most of the rest of us work for wages—if and when capitalists will hire us.

Now the power and prestige of a capitalist are, generally speaking, in proportion to his wealth, and it follows that his main object in life is and must be to get richer than he is. He therefore operates his business in such a way as to make the greatest possible profit, and he takes a good part of that profit and adds it to his capital. The process goes on and on; there is no end to it. With all the capitalists doing the same thing, the natural result is that all their businesses, which is another way of saying the total social means of production, tend to expand at the same time and without limit.

But it is obvious that society's capacity to produce cannot be expanded indefinitely and without reference to the size of the final market for consumer goods. Sooner or later the result is bound to be "overproduction"—piling up of unsold goods in the hands of retailers and wholesalers, collapse of prices, shrinkage or disappearance of

---

*This article originally appeared in* Welfare State: the Twenty-Fourth Annual Debate Handbook *of the National University Extension Association, copyright* 1950, *and is reprinted by special permission.*

profits, and finally a stagnation of production coupled with heavy unemployment. After a while, stocks will be sold off, durable consumer goods (like automobiles and refrigerators) will wear out, and factories will begin to need new machinery to keep up even a low level of production. Then things pick up again, and the merry chase for more profits and more capital is resumed.

That's the way the system works. It's a system of booms and busts—not by accident or because of some superficial defect, but by its very nature. Moreover, the more advanced a capitalist country is, that is to say, the more highly developed its productive resources and the richer its capitalists, the weaker will be the booms and the more devastating the busts.

The United States is the most advanced capitalist country in the world. Its major problem is how to keep bust, or in other words low production and high unemployment, from being the normal state of the national economy.

During the 1930's it *was* the normal state of the national economy. Despite strenuous efforts on the part of the federal government (efforts which included extraordinary expenditures for doles, work relief, and public works), the period was one of persistent and massive unemployment. No one knows how many were unemployed at the bottom of the depression in 1932-33, but the figure was certainly more than 15 million; and in only one year (1937) did unemployment fall below 10 million.

World War II saved American capitalism. It put everyone to work and doubled productive capacity and brought undreamed-of wealth to the big corporations and capitalists.

Many people, including some very able economists, predicted that soon after the war was over there would be another bust and the old problem of the 30's would be back with us again. It has not worked out that way, however. The reason is not that the capitalist system has changed its nature but that the cold war has taken the place of the hot war as the dominant factor in the American economy. Cold war is not as expensive as hot war, and it does not keep the productive machine going at the same break-neck speed. But the $20 billion a year which are currently being spent on arms and on foreign aid programs have so far been enough to hold off the bust and to keep unemployment from being much above the 5-million mark.[1]

The result is that the whole capitalist class now has a vested interest in keeping the cold war going—and in warming it up and making it more expensive if necessary. And the capitalists have the

---

[1] *This was written early in 1950. Now, nearly two decades later, the figure is more than $78 billion and still rising.*

means to keep it going, too. They control the press, the radio and television, the movies, schools and colleges; their representatives sit in the halls of Congress and in the key positions in the State and Defense Departments. They systematically spread stories of impending Russian aggression, of Communist spies, and of subversive plots to overthrow the United States government. They whip up mass hysteria which provides the proper atmosphere of intolerance, bigotry, and bellicosity in which the cold war, with all its blessings to American capitalism, can be fought to the limit.

This is not the place to discuss American foreign policy or to examine the reality behind the "Russian menace"; but one thing is sure, and that is that if we are ever to bring the cold war to an end, if we are ever to establish a world in which we can live in peace and security, we must reform the American economy so that prosperity is no longer completely dependent on war or war preparations.

That is the number one problem of an economic program for America.

There are many other problems, some closely related to the number one problem, some overlapping it, some relatively independent. It is obviously impossible, in a brief essay, to discuss them all. I shall therefore limit attention to the few that seem to me to be most important and that every one must surely agree are of major national concern.

(2) How to achieve a fairer and saner distribution of income.

(3) How to provide for the welfare and security of the aged, the sick, and all others who, for whatever reason, are unable to provide for their own livelihood.

(4) How to eliminate the overbearing power of private monopoly to exploit the worker, the consumer, and the farmer.

(5) How to conserve and husband our natural resources.

(6) How to eliminate the enormous waste entailed in our present system of production and distribution (for example, the employment of brains, manpower, and resources in the wholly wasteful business of competitive advertising and salesmanship) and to realize the full potentialities of modern science and technology for the benefit not only of the American people but also of other countries which are economically and technically less advanced.

I am convinced that not a single one of these problems can be satisfactorily solved within the framework of a capitalist economy. On the other hand, their solution flows easily and naturally from the adoption of one master reform: the socialization of the means of production (except those which are actually used by their owners) with its inevitable corollary, the introduction of overall economic planning.

## II

A socialized and planned economy—in other words, the economic system which is known as socialism—functions according to principles and laws which are very different from those which govern a capitalist system. The individual productive and trading units are not operated with a view to the maximization of profit; their aim is to fulfill the tasks which are prescribed for them in the national economic plan. Under capitalism an industrialist is successful in proportion to the amount of money he makes for himself or for the stockholders he represents; under socialism he is successful to the degree that the plant which has been entrusted to his management carries out the tasks which society assigns to it through the medium of the plan.

This is a crucial difference. It means that the basic tendency of capitalism which we already noticed, that is to say, the tendency for society's aggregate means of production to expand without limit and without reference to the size of the final market for consumer goods, does not and cannot manifest itself under socialism. Under both systems, society's productive forces are (or at any rate can be) known with a reasonable degree of accuracy. The difference is that under capitalism the allocation of these resources—and especially the division between those that are to produce more means of production and those that are to produce consumer goods—is the outcome of millions of decisions of capitalists acting in their own interest and independently of each other; while under socialism the allocation of resources is planned in advance to satisfy consciously felt social needs.

This is not to say that a socialist economy would never make any mistakes: that would be foolish. But it is to say that a socialist economy would always and as a matter of course strive to adjust the expansion of the means of production to the requirements of the people's rising consumption needs (including, of course, such collective needs as highways, education, and national defense). Mistakes would always take place within the framework of a planned and balanced economy and could always be rectified without the danger of precipitating a general depression. And as experience and skill in making and executing national economic plans grew, mistakes would naturally become less and less important.

What this means is that socialism *by its very nature* solves the central dilemma of a capitalist economy. There is simply no problem of boom and bust, of unemployment, of stagnant production under socialism. There is no need for a special program to eliminate the business cycle or to combat depressions. These economic disasters are specific products of capitalism, and only a capitalist system has to worry about what to do about them. It follows, of course, that prosperity under socialism could *never* be dependent on war or war preparations. In a planned economy, such activities would directly and obviously appear as what they are, the unfortunate and impoverishing diversion of resources from purposes of construction to purposes of destruction.

## III

At this point, however, a fundamental question arises. The American people, it may be argued, are not ready for socialism. Must we not therefore devote our energies to solving the problem within the framework of capitalism? And have not the theorists of what has been called the "New Economics"—that is to say, the school founded by the late English economist, John Maynard Keynes —shown us how the problem can in fact be solved within the framework of capitalism?

In order to answer this question, we must indicate very briefly the nature of the solution recommended by the Keynesians. Without entering into their underlying theories, we can perhaps best convey the nature of their reasoning by quoting a question which Stuart Chase says was asked of him during the war by a GI tank driver on his way to France: "Well, if the country can keep prosperous making tanks for men like us to die in, why can't it keep prosperous making houses for people to live in?"[2] The Keynesians answer that the country can do just that—with the understanding that in this context the term "houses" includes all sorts of constructive projects in the fields of education, welfare, resource conservation, public utilities, and even industry. Thus the Keynesians would say that if the economy is now being maintained in a satisfactory state of prosperity by roughly $20 billion of cold-war spending, it would likewise be kept in that state by $20 billion of what might be called "welfare-state" spending. Hence if America is now dependent on cold war for its prosperity this is only because of a lack of understanding. Capitalism can be made to work well enough, according to this view, if the people and their representatives will only abandon old-fashioned economic orthodoxy and allow the government—through its borrowing and taxing policies on the one hand and its lending and spending policies on the other—to become the balance wheel of the economy in peacetime as well as in wartime.

The answer to the Keynesians does not lie in the realm of abstract economic theory. *If* an American capitalist government could spend $20 billion—and if necessary $30 billion or $40 billion—for peaceful, constructive purposes, then the Keynesians would doubtless be right. But the point is precisely that the ruling capitalist class, the very class

---

2 *"If Peace Breaks Out,"* The Nation, *June* 11, 1949, *p.* 656.

whose enormous wealth and power is assured by the structure of capitalism itself, will never approve or permit spending on this scale (or anything even approaching this scale) for peaceful, constructive ends. Nor is this a matter of ignorance or stupidity. It is a plain matter of class interest, which, to the capitalist class (as to all ruling classes in history), appears to be the national interest and indeed the interest of civilization itself.

Take housing, for example. Why not a gigantic program to rebuild and rehouse America? Heaven knows, we need it badly enough! But every one who has passed the age of ten knows the answer: the real estate interests. They will put up with a small amount of government housing, preferably in the field of slum clearance; but when it comes to anything big they say NO and they get the solid backing of all the propertied interests of the country.

Or take social security. Why not a real social security program? Here again, there is no lack of need. But a real social security program would involve a considerable degree of income redistribution from rich to poor. And besides, capitalists do not *want* too much security—for others. It is bad for morale, dulls the incentive to work, leads to exaggerated expectations and pretensions. Capitalists believe —and not without reason—that their system requires enormous rewards at the top and poverty and insecurity at the bottom to keep it going. A real social security program contradicts both these requirements and will therefore always be opposed to the limit by the capitalist class.

Or take government investment in industry or public utilities or transportation. There is no end of useful projects which government could undertake at any given time—IF it were free to compete with private enterprise. But of course government is not free to compete with private enterprise; in fact it is here that the resistance of the capitalists to the extension of government activities is at the maximum. They regard all branches of the economy that can be made to yield a profit as their own private preserve at the entrance to which they have posted a a huge "No Trespassing" sign. If anything seems certain it is that as long as we have capitalism we shall have very little government investment in the production of useful *and saleable* goods and services.

And so it goes. To every form of peaceful, constructive government spending the capitalists have an objection: it redistributes income, or it increases the power and independence of the working class, or it competes with private enterprise. A New Deal government, enjoying overwhelming popular support, may be able to make some headway against these objections; but as long as the capitalists have the levers of economic power in their hands, they will be able to block, or if necessary sabotage, any program which would make the government the balance wheel in an expanding peace economy.

It is very different in the case of spending for military purposes. The flow of orders for armaments benefits the biggest capitalist monopolies; there is no competition with private enterprise; and the whole atmosphere of a cold war—the witch hunts, the jingoism, the worship of force—creates the conditions in which the ruling class finds it easiest to control the ideas and the activities of the underlying population.

And so we must tell the "realists" who urge the necessity of working within the framework of capitalism that they are being hopelessly unrealistic. It is not possible to maintain a system that guarantees wealth and power to capitalists and at the same time to make it work in ways to which they are irrevocably opposed. If the American people are not ready for socialism—and it can hardly be denied that they are not—then the real realist will recognize that the most urgent task of our time is to get them ready.

## IV

So much for our number one problem. Let us now turn very briefly to the other problems on our list. We shall find in each case (a) that they are insoluble under capitalism, and (b) that there are no inherent obstacles to their rational solution under socialism.

*Income Distribution.* The real reason for the grossly unequal and unfair distribution of income in America today is private ownership of the means of production. About two-thirds of our national income is paid out in the form of wages and salaries and about one-third in the form of profit, interest, and rent. Most of this latter one-third goes to a relatively very small proportion of the population, and it is this fact that gives the distribution of income as a whole its characteristic shape.[3]

---

[3] *Statisticians have devised an index of inequality which would stand at zero in case of perfect equality (that is, if every one's income were the same) and at one in case of perfect inequality (that is, if one individual had all the income and every one else had nothing). Thus the lower the index the greater the equality, and the higher the index the greater the inequality. Calculations based on 1945 federal income tax returns show that wages and salaries (with an index of .38) are much more equally distributed than business and partnership income (.68) on the one hand and than interest and dividend income (.82) on the other. Selma F. Goldsmith, "Statistical Information on the Distribution of Income by Size in the United States,"* Papers and Proceedings of the 62nd Annual Meeting of the American Economic Association, *p. 327.*

The experience of Great Britain strongly suggests that this situation cannot be fundamentally changed within the framework of a capitalist economy.[4] It seems to be pretty generally agreed that the Labor government in Britain has gone about as far as it is possible to go in the direction of taxing the rich while still maintaining a private-enterprise economy. But even so, as the following table shows, the fundamental distribution of income between labor and property did not change much between 1938 and 1948 and does not differ greatly from the ratio of two-thirds to one-third which obtains in the United States. (And there have been no significant changes since.)

DISTRIBUTION OF INCOME IN U. K., 1938 AND 1948*

|  | % Before Taxes 1938 | 1948 | % After Direct Taxes 1938 | 1948 | % After All Taxes 1938 | 1948 |
|---|---|---|---|---|---|---|
| Labor | 61 | 60 | 64 | 65 | 63 | 63 |
| Property | 38 | 38 | 34 | 32 | 35 | 34 |
| Armed Forces | 1 | 2 | 2 | 3 | 2 | 3 |
| Total | 100 | 100 | 100 | 100 | 100 | 100 |

Socialism, of course, solves this problem automatically by doing away with private property in the means of production and placing at the disposal of society as a whole the income (as we have seen, roughly one-third of the total) which now goes to the relatively small class of capitalists.

*Social Security.* Not much needs to be added on this subject to what has already been said above. As long as capitalists have the power they will use it to oppose the building up of a really adequate social security system. This does not mean, however, that nothing can be accomplished under capitalism. Unsatisfactory as our present social security system is, it is nevertheless much better than what we had twenty years ago; and the experience of other capitalist countries

---

4 *Contrary to a widely held belief, Britain today is still a capitalist country. At the present time about six-sevenths of all employment in the U. K., excluding only the normal functions of government, is in private firms and only about one-seventh in socialized firms. See P. M. Sweezy,* Socialism *(McGraw-Hill, 1949), pp. 45-47. It is true that the Labor government has actively and extensively intervened in the British economy in the last five years, but it has done so in response to immediate problems and emergencies, not in accordance with an overall plan. We must always remember that—as an anonymous British writer has put it—"making life difficult for capitalism is not the same thing, by any means, as transforming it into socialism." "British Labor and Socialism,"* Monthly Review, *Sept. 1949, p. 143.*

*Computed from figures given in the official White Paper on National Income and Expenditure of the U. K., 1946-48 (Cmd. 7649).

## AN ECONOMIC PROGRAM FOR AMERICA

—chief among them the Scandinavian countries, New Zealand, Australia, and Britain—proves that much more can be done in this line than the major American political parties have yet been willing even to consider. Hence all liberals and radicals will as a matter of course consistently press for improvements in our social security system. But this does not in any way change our conclusion that progress will ultimately require the effective elimination of the capitalists' power to oppose and obstruct.

*Monopoly.* Almost everyone agrees that the monopoly problem arises from two closely interrelated causes: large-scale production and the combination of many productive units under unified corporate managements. Big production units and even bigger management units have long since become the characteristic feature of the industries which dominate American economic life. Almost everyone—except, no doubt, the big businessmen themselves—also agrees that something should be done about the monopoly problem, that the degree of concentration which now exists is both economically and politically dangerous.

One common proposal is that the antitrust laws should be more vigorously enforced. But this is precisely what has been happening in recent years. Mr. Herbert A. Bergson, chief of the Anti-trust Division of the Department of Justice, told the Celler Committee that

> more cases have been instituted in the last 10 years than in the entire 50 years before that. Our record of wins against losses in the courts has been most impressive. Nor do the court cases tell the whole story. Approximately 25 percent of our cases result in consent judgments, in which relief against illegal practices is obtained without the necessity of going to trial. Finally . . . the mere existence of the anti-trust laws, coupled with the knowledge that violations will be punished, has a tremendous influence in keeping our economy democratic and competitive.[5]

And yet despite all this activity and these many victories, witness after witness testified to the growth of monopoly in the last ten years. The inference is plain, that the anti-trust laws are powerless to deal with the situation. And it follows that to advocate relying on them is merely another way of opposing any effective action on the monopoly problem.

A second approach to the monopoly problem would establish

---

[5] *The Celler Committee was a subcommittee of the House Judiciary Committee which conducted extensive hearings in the late 1940's and 1950's and published the results in many volumes under the general title,* Study of Monopoly Power. *This quotation is from Part I, p. 381.*

regulatory commissions, on the model of the Interstate Commerce Commission and the various state public utility commissions, to control the activities of the large concentrated industries. There are, however, many and compelling objections to this proposal. Commission regulation has proved itself to be unwieldy and inefficient; it spawns red tape and bureaucracy in the worst sense of the terms; and the commissions always end by becoming the friend and backer of the private industries they are supposed to regulate rather than the protector of the public interest.[6] Regulatory commissions are no more effective than anti-trust laws as a method of dealing with the monopoly problem, and they are likely to do a great deal more harm.

Finally, it is often urged that the solution of the monopoly problem is to be found in a new approach which would enforce competition through putting a limit on the size of firms. Those who advocate this method, however, are obliged to admit that the proposed maximum size would have to be different in different industries. Hence it would be necessary to establish a commission to determine the permissible limit in each industry; and after the commission had made its findings each case would have to go through the courts. This would be merely an extension of traditional anti-trust procedure. It could be expected to lead to endless litigation, weighty pronouncements by the Supreme Court, perhaps a few highly publicized splitting-up actions—and for the rest a more secure tenure for monopoly because some of the pressure "to do something about it" would have been removed. But even if this method would work it would be highly objectionable. Big business, on the whole, is efficiently and expertly conducted. To attempt to solve the monopoly problem by pulverizing big business would be like throwing out the baby with the bath.

The trouble with big business under capitalism is not that it is big but that it is private and socially irresponsible. The remedy for that is obvious: make it public and socially responsible.

*Natural Resources.* There is writ large in the annals of American history the lesson that private enterprise is wasteful and destructive of natural resources, that government regulation is at best nega-

---

[6] *Note the following statement of former Governor Ellis Arnall of Georgia to the Celler Committee: ". . . since those regulatory bodies dealt only really with the people they regulated, through the course of years, since politics cost money at the state level where they run for reelection and at the federal level where pressures are not unknown, very soon we find ourselves with an amazing situation whereby many of these regulatory bodies . . . exist not to protect the public, but to stand as a bulwark against the public to protect the people they regulate." Ibid., Part I, p. 268.*

tively effective, and that social ownership and planning are not only effective but yield positive results out of all proportion to the costs involved. The case of timber will serve to illustrate the comparison. The ruthless cutting-over of our forests by private capitalists had to be stopped by government action, but only where far-reaching government ownership and planning have been instituted—most notably in the case of the TVA—has it been possible to evolve a rational forestry policy as a part of a comprehensive program of conserving and developing our natural resources.

Another industry, coal mining, underscores the point. Coal is a sick industry, losing its markets to competing fuels, throwing out of work more and more miners who find it practically impossible to move into other occupations, and beset by periodic labor disputes which each time threaten the economic life of the country. This is a problem which private enterprise and government regulation alike are powerless to cope with. It requires for its solution much more radical action: nothing less than the scrapping of private enterprise—not only in coal but also in oil and natural gas and all the other fuels which provide the lifeblood of modern industrial society—and the substitution of social enterprise operating in accordance with a long-run plan of conservation and development.

*The Wastefulness of Capitalism.* The real wastefulness of capitalism certainly does not lie in the organization of its big corporations, as many well-meaning reformers seem to believe; nor, in the final analysis, even in its undoubted prodigality with our heritage of natural resources. It lies rather in the structure and functioning of the system as a whole—in the making of exquisite luxuries for a few while millions are condemned to misery and poverty; in misdirecting brains and energy and resources into the insanities of competitive salesmanship; in the foregone production and the blighted lives of depression; in the destruction and slaughter of wars to divide and redivide the world; and now in the monstrous waste of a cold war to preserve the *status quo* at home and abroad.

In its day, capitalism was a progressive system. It created the productive forces which have completely revolutionized the world we live in. Its big corporations are in many ways models of rational and efficient organization. But capitalism does not know how to utilize constructively what it has created; it is like the sorcerer who could not control the forces of the nether world which he called up by his spell. If we are to enjoy the benefits of modern science and technology, if we are really to help others and not merely exploit them under the pretense of helping them, we must get rid of this blind, socially wasteful, destructive system, and we must put in its place a system which permits rational intelligence and common sense to play a role not only in the lives of individuals but also in the life of society as a whole.

# LESSONS OF SOVIET EXPERIENCE
## BY LEO HUBERMAN AND PAUL M. SWEEZY

Anniversaries are traditionally a time for celebration, and there is indeed much to celebrate on this anniversary of the Revolution which overthrew not only the *ancien regime* but the whole system of capitalism in Russia 50 years ago this month.

Never before had a revolutionary leadership acted with such profound historical insight, with such bold decisiveness, with such a perfect sense of timing. What had seemed to many the empty boast that Marxism was a science of revolution was triumphantly vindicated by Lenin and his fellow Bolsheviks in 1917.

Never before had a working class become the ruling class of a great country, and never had any revolutionary class fought more tenaciously and courageously against as formidable a coalition of domestic and foreign enemies.

Never before had such radical and irreversible changes in the structure of a society been effected in so short a time.

But perhaps most important, never before had a revolution had such repercussions or evoked popular interest and sympathy on a world-wide scale. The American and French Revolutions of the 18th century shook Europe and its overseas offshoots to their foundations but left the rest of the world, by far the largest part of the world in both population and territory, largely untouched. It was precisely this largest part of the world that the October Revolution at long last stirred into motion and pushed onto the long and arduous road of social transformation. Before 1917 Marxism and socialism were essentially European phenomena; after 1917 they rapidly developed into the only universal ideological and political movement the world has ever known.

*From the November, 1967 issue of* MONTHLY REVIEW, *published on the occasion of the 50th anniversary of the Russian Revolution. The issue is now available in a Monthly Review Press book entitled* Fifty Years of Soviet Power.

"I have been over into the future and it works," said Lincoln Steffens after a visit to Russia in 1918. Never were truer or more prophetic words spoken. The October Revolution marked the birth of the historical era of socialism, and for this supreme achievement we celebrate it today as mankind will continue to celebrate it for centuries to come.

But there is more to celebrate too. Historically speaking, 50 years are a very short time; and it could easily have happened that during its first half century socialism might have made little headway or might even have been temporarily crushed in its birthplace by the forces of international counter-revolution. That this did not happen, that instead socialism spread in little more than three decades to vast new areas of the earth, is due in very large part to the unprecedentedly rapid industrialization of the Soviet Union in the late 1920's and the 1930's. If this massive industrialization had not been successfully carried through in time, the Soviet Union would have lacked the economic and military strength to withstand the Nazi onslaught of 1941; and the revival of socialism within the USSR and its spread to other lands might not have occurred for many years. Nearly two decades of forced industrialization and total war cost the people of the USSR more than 20 million lives and untold suffering. But these heavy sacrifices were not in vain, nor were those who made them the only beneficiaries. By timely preparation and heroic struggle, the Soviet Union played the decisive role in smashing the fascist bid for world power and thereby kept the road open for the second great advance of socialism in the period after 1945. For these historic achievements no less than for the October Revolution itself, mankind owes a lasting debt of gratitude to the Soviet Union and its people.

Spokesmen for the Soviet regime both at home and abroad claim yet another achievement which they believe mankind should celebrate on this 50th anniversary. The Soviet Union, they say, has not only laid the foundations of socialism through nationalizing the means of production, building up industry, and collectivizing agriculture; it has also gone far toward erecting on these foundations the socialist edifice itself—a society such as Marx and Lenin envisaged, still tainted by its bourgeois origins but steadily improving and already well along the road to the ultimate goal of full communism. If this were true, it certainly

# LESSONS OF SOVIET EXPERIENCE

should be celebrated, perhaps more enthusiastically than any of the other achievements of the first half century of Soviet existence. For then we should know that, at least in principle, mankind has already solved its most fundamental problems and that what is needed now is only time for the Soviet Union to work the solutions out to their ultimate consequences, and determination and will on the part of the rest of the world to follow the Soviet example.

If only it were true! But, alas, apart from the pronouncements of the ideologists and admirers of the Soviet regime, it is extremely difficult to find supporting evidence; while the accumulation of evidence pointing to a quite different conclusion is as persuasive as it is massive.

The facts indicate that relative to most other countries in the world today, the Soviet Union is a stable society with an enormously powerful state apparatus and an economy capable of reasonably rapid growth for the foreseeable future. It is also a stratified society, with a deep chasm between the ruling stratum of political bureaucrats and economic managers on the one side and the mass of working people on the other, and an impressive spectrum of income and status differentials on both sides of the chasm. The society appears to be effectively depoliticized at all levels, hence *a fortiori* non-revolutionary. In these circumstances the concerns and motivations of individuals and families are naturally focused on private affairs and in particular on individual careers and family consumption levels. Moreover since the economy is able to provide both an abundance of career openings and a steadily expanding supply of consumer goods, these private motivations are effective in shaping the quantity, quality, allocation, and discipline of the labor force. There is probably no capitalist country in the world today, with the possible exception of Japan, in which classical bourgeois mechanisms operate as efficiently to secure the kinds and amounts of work needed to propel the economy forward.

But the prevalence of these mechanisms, and indeed their very success, cannot but have a profound influence on the quality of the society and the "human nature" of its members. This is part of the ABC of socialist thought and need not be elaborated upon here: suffice it to say that the privatization of economic life leads necessarily to the privatization of social life and the evisceration of political life. Bourgeois values, bourgeois criteria of success, bourgeois modes of behavior are fostered. Politics becomes a specialty, a branch of the division of labor, like any other career. And of course the other side of the coin is the perpetuation and deepening of that alienation of man from his fellows and hence from himself which many socialists have long felt to be the ultimate evil of bourgeois society.

It may be argued that while these tendencies exist—this, we believe, can be denied only by blind apologists—they are not yet dominant and they are being effectively offset by counter-tendencies. In this connection, it is usual to cite, as Maurice Dobb does in his recent essay,* the narrowing of the gap in incomes and living standards between the collective-farm peasantry and the urban proletariat, the leveling-up of the lower end of wage and pension scales, the shortening of the working day, and a general rise in living standards. These developments are supposed to be preparing the way for a transformation of the social consciousness and morality of the Soviet people. As William Pomeroy explained, after an extensive tour around the Soviet Union:

> The Soviet view is that education in communist behavior can go only so far without continually rising living standards. They say they are now "laying the material base for communism," and that the aim is to create the highest living standards in the world and that the "new man" will fully flourish only under conditions of abundance.**

What this argument overlooks is that living standards are not only a matter of quantity but also of quality. With negligible exceptions, all Marxists and socialists recognize the necessity of high and rising living standards to the realization of socialist goals and the transition to communism. But this is the beginning of the problem not the end. It should be obvious by now from the experience of the advanced capitalist countries that higher living standards based on the accumulation of goods for private use—houses, automobiles, appliances, apparel, jewelry, etc.—do not create a "new man"; on the contrary, they tend to bring out the worst in the "old man," stimulating greed and selfishness in the economically more fortunate and envy and hatred in the less fortunate. In these circumstances no amount of "edu-

---

\* "The October Revolution and Half a Century," *Fifty Years of Soviet Power*, p. 38.
\*\* *National Guardian*, July 8, 1967.

cation in communist behavior"—as practiced, shall we say, by the ecclesiastical establishments of Western Christendom—can do more than provide a thin disguise for the ugly reality.

But is any other kind of rising living standards, more compatible with the realization of socialist goals, conceivable? The answer is obviously yes. We may concede that a priority charge on a socialist society's increasing production is to provide leaders and more skilled and/or responsible workers with what they need to do their jobs properly. But beyond that certain principles could be followed: (1) Private needs and wants should be satisfied only at a level at which they can be satisfied for all. (2) Production of such goods and services should be increased only if and when the increments are large and divisible enough to go around. (3) All other increases in the production of consumer goods should be for collective consumption. As applied to an underdeveloped country, these principles mean that there should be no production of automobiles, household appliances, or other consumer durable goods for private sale and use. The reason is simply that to turn out enough such products to go around would require many years, perhaps even many decades, and if they are distributed privately in the meantime the result can only be to create or aggravate glaring material inequalities. The appropriate socialist policy is therefore to produce these types of goods in forms and quantities best suited to the collective satisfaction of needs: car pools, communal cooking and eating establishments, apartment-house or neighborhood laundries, and so on. Such a policy, it should be emphasized, would mean not only a different *utilization* of goods but also a very different pattern of production. In the case of automobiles in particular, a policy of production for collective needs means a strictly limited production, since for many purposes the automobile is an inefficient and irrational means of transportation. Furthermore, restricting the output of automobiles and concentrating instead on other forms of transportation requires a different pattern of investment in highways, railroads, subways, airports, and so on.

Now, if the Soviets had embarked upon a program of raising living standards in this second, socialist sense, there would be every reason to take seriously the contention that, certain appearances to the contrary notwithstanding, they are indeed "laying the material base for communism." But this is certainly not the case, nor could it be the case as long as Soviet society is geared to and dependent upon a system of private incentives.* These matters are all indissolubly tied together. A depoliticized society *must* rely on private incentives; and for private incentives to work effectively, the structure of production *must* be shaped to turn out the goods and services which give the appropriate concrete meaning to money incomes and demands. The only way out of this seemingly closed circle would be a *re*politicization of Soviet society which would permit a move away from private incentives and hence also a different structure of production and a different composition and distribution of additions to the social product. But repoliticization would also mean much else, including in particular a radical change in the present leadership and its methods of governing—at least a "cultural revolution," if not something even more drastic. This means that short of a major upheaval, which does not seem likely in the foreseeable future, the present course is set for a long time to come. And since, as we have already indicated, this course has little to do with "laying the material base for communism," we have to ask in what direction it is leading.

The answer, we believe, is that it is leading to a hardening of material inequalities in Soviet society. The process by which this is occurring can be seen most clearly in the area of consumer durable goods. For most of Soviet history, the need to concentrate on heavy industry and war production, and to devote most of consumer goods production to meeting the elementary requirements of the mass of the population, precluded the possibility of developing industries catering to the latent demand of the higher-income strata for consumer durables. In respect to this aspect of the standard of living, which bulks so large in the advanced capitalist countries, there was therefore a sort of enforced equality in the Soviet Union. In the last few years, how-

---

* The debate over incentives is usually couched in terms of "material" vs. "moral." But this is not really accurate, since in both cases material gains are envisaged: the opposition lies rather in the composition of the gains and the way they are distributed. Hence it may be more helpful to speak of "private" vs. "collective" incentives. At the same time it should be recognized that there *is* a moral element in the collective incentive system: behavior directed toward improving the lot of everyone (including oneself) is certainly more moral, and presupposes a higher level of social consciousness, than behavior directed toward immediate private gain.

## LESSONS OF SOVIET EXPERIENCE

ever, this situation has been changing. Now at last the production of refrigerators, washing machines, automobiles, etc. on an increasing scale has become feasible, and the Soviet government is moving vigorously to develop this sector of the economy. And while a considerable proportion of the output, especially in the case of the automobile industry, will have to be devoted to official and public uses for years to come, nevertheless it is clear that the basic policy is to channel a larger and larger share of consumer durable production into the private market. Some idea of what this portends is conveyed by Harrison Salisbury in an article entitled "A Balance Sheet of 50 Years of Soviet Rule" in the *New York Times* of October 2, 1967:

> In the 50th year of Bolshevik power the Soviet Union stands on the edge of the automobile age that the United States entered in the 1920's. With new production facilities being constructed by Fiat, Renault, and others, the Soviet Union will be turning out 1,500,000 passenger cars a year in the early 1970's, more than five times the present output. But this will not be soon enough to cut off the wave of popular grumbling.
> 
> "When I see that any ordinary worker in Italy or France has a car," said a writer just back from one of his frequent trips to Western Europe, "I wonder what we have been doing in the last 50 years. Of course, there has been progress. But it's not fast enough."
> 
> The Soviet Union's entry into the automobile age is not going to be easy. The Russian writer owns a car, a 10-year-old Pobeda. He has to keep it on the street all winter in temperatures of 30 below zero. No garages are available. None are provided in the new apartments or office buildings. Most Moscow car owners drain their radiators every night in winter and fill them in the morning with boiling water to get started. There are three gasoline stations in Moscow selling high-test gasoline. Today there are perhaps 100,000 private cars in Moscow. What will happen when there are a million?

Part of the answer of course is that along with the increase in production of cars, the Soviet Union will have to embark on a vast expansion in the provision of all the facilities required by an automobilized society: highways, garages, service stations, parking lots, motels, and all the rest. And in sum, if American experience is a reliable indicator, these complements to the automobile will absorb an even larger part of the Soviet economy's labor power and material resources than production of the vehicles themselves.

Two points need to be specially emphasized. First, even assuming a continued rapid increase in automobile production, it will be many, many years before more than a small minority of the Soviet population can hope to join the ranks of car owners. During this period, the automobile will add a new dimension to the structure of material inequality in Soviet society, which will by no means be limited to the simple possession of cars. Those who have their own private means of mobility tend to develop a distinctive style of life. The automobile increasingly dominates their use of leisure time (after work hours, weekends, vacations) and thus indirectly generates a whole new set of needs, ranging from country houses for those who can afford them through camping equipment to all kinds of sporting goods.

Second, and this is a point which is generally neglected but which in our view is of crucial importance, the allocation of vast quantities of human and material resources to the production of private consumer durable goods and their complementary facilities means neglecting or holding back the development of other sectors of the economy and society. Or to put the matter more bluntly: A society which decides to go in for private consumer durables in a big way at the same time decides *not* to make the raising of mass living standards its number one priority.* And these are indeed the decisions which the Soviet leadership has taken and is in the process of vigorously implementing.

To sum up: The course on which the Soviet Union has embarked implies a long period of *increased* material inequality during which productive resources are, directly and indirectly, channeled into satisfying the wants of a privileged minority and mass living standards are raised less rapidly and less fully than would otherwise be possible.

We shall perhaps be told that even if the period in question is of necessity long, it is in principle transitional and will eventually lead, via a process of leveling-up, to a situation in which

---

* With this in mind, we can see how absurd it is to describe the debate between Soviet spokesmen and their critics in the socialist camp as being between those who want the Soviet people to have "the good things of life" and those who would impose on them an artificial austerity. The truth is that it is between those who want a small minority to have the lion's share of the good things and those who think these good things ought to be produced and distributed in forms accessible to the broad masses.

everyone is a full participant in a society of consumer-durable-goods abundance—or, in other words (since the automobile is by far the dominant consumer durable), to a fully automobilized society. It is a strange conception of socialism, this gadget utopia; but, fortunately or unfortunately, it does not seem very likely to be realized. For if anything is well established on the basis of long and varied historical experience, it is that a ruling stratum which is firmly rooted in power and has accustomed itself to the enjoyment of privileges and emoluments finds ways to preserve and protect its vested interests against mass invasion from below. There already exists such a ruling stratum in the Soviet Union, and the course now being followed guarantees that its privileged position will be enhanced and strengthened for a long time to come. If anyone thinks this stratum is going to renounce its position unless obliged to do so by *force majeure*, he is either a dreamer or a believer in miracles. "Laying the material base for communism" seems to be a slogan of the same kind as those even more famous slogans of the 18th-century bourgeois revolutions—"life, liberty, and the pursuit of happiness" and "liberté, egalité, fraternité"—designed to rally the support of those who look forward to a better future but increasingly divorced from economic and social reality.

The reader will note that we have been careful to speak of a ruling "stratum" rather than a ruling "class." The difference is that the members of a stratum can stem from diverse social origins, while the great majority (though not all) of the members of a class are born into it. A new class usually begins as a stratum and only hardens into a class after several generations during which privileges become increasingly hereditary and barriers are erected to upward mobility. Historically, property systems have been the most common institutional arrangement for ensuring the inheritability of privilege and blocking the upward movement of the unprivileged. But other devices such as caste and hereditary nobility have also served these purposes.

To what extent, if at all, the Soviet system of stratification has developed into a true class system we do not pretend to know. Fifty years—about two generations by usual calculations—is in any case too short a time for the crystalization of such a profound social change. At the present time, therefore, one can only say that conditions favoring the development of a class system exist and that in the absence of effective counter-forces, we must assume that these conditions will bear their natural fruit. And by effective counter-forces we do not mean ideological doctrines or statements of good intentions but organized political struggle. Unless or until signs of such struggle appear, one can only conclude that Soviet stratification will in due course be transformed into a new class system.

That all this is a far cry from the Marxian vision of the future (even the relatively near-term post-revolutionary future) as expressed for example in Marx's *Critique of the Gotha Program* or Lenin's *State and Revolution,* needs no demonstration. This divergence between theory and practice will naturally be interpreted by bourgeois critics as (yet another) proof of the failure of Marxism and as (further) evidence that "you can't change human nature." What is the Marxian answer to these critics? Did it have to happen that way in the Soviet Union? Or might events have taken a different course there? These are by no means mere "academic" questions (i.e. questions the answers to which have no practical significance). If what has happened in the Soviet Union had to happen, the chances that other socialist countries, present and future, will be able to escape the same fate would, at the very least, have to be rated low. If on the other hand events might have taken a different course in the Soviet Union, then other socialist countries, learning from Soviet experience, can still hope to prove that Marx and Lenin were right after all and that in entering the era of socialism mankind has at last found the key to a new and qualitatively better future.

What is at issue here is really the age-old question of historical determinism. The determinist position holds essentially that the conditions which exist at any given time uniquely determine what will happen next. This does not necessarily mean that every individual's thoughts and actions are uniquely determined, but only that in the given circumstances only one combination of thoughts and actions can be effectively put into practice. Individuals can choose but societies cannot. At the other extreme, what is often called the voluntarist position holds that anything can happen depending on the will and determination of key individuals or groups.

Marxism is neither determinist nor voluntarist; or, if you prefer, it is both determinist and voluntarist. "Men make their own history," wrote Marx in the second paragraph of the

*Eighteenth Brumaire of Louis Bonaparte,* "but they do not make it just as they please; they do not make it under circumstances chosen by themselves, but under circumstances directly encountered, given and transmitted from the past" In other words, at any given time the range of possibilities is determined by what has gone before (determinism), but within this range genuine choices are possible (voluntarism). This very general principle, however, by no means exhausts the Marxian position. Even more important from our present point of view is the idea, which is of the very essence of Marxism as a revolutionary doctrine, that in the life of societies there are long periods of relative stability during which a given social order unfolds and finally reaches the end of its potentialities, and that these are followed by periods of revolutionary transition to a new social order. This theme is of course familiar to all students of Marxism, especially from the famous Preface to the *Critique of Political Economy.* What does not seem to have been widely recognized is the clear implication that the ratio of determinism to voluntarism in historical explanation necessarily varies greatly from one period to another. Once a social order is firmly established and its "law of motion" is in full operation, power naturally gravitates into the hands of those who understand the system's requirements and are willing and able to act as its agents and beneficiaries. In these circumstances, there is little that individuals or groups can do to change the course of history: for the time being a strictly deterministic doctrine seems to be fully vindicated. But when the inherent contradictions of the system have had time to mature and the objective conditions for a revolutionary transformation have come into existence, then the situation changes radically. The system's law of motion breaks down wholly or in part, class struggles grow in intensity, and crises multiply. Under these circumstances the range of possibilities widens, and groups (especially, in our time, disciplined political parties) and great leaders come into their own as actors on the stage of history. Determinism recedes into the background, and voluntarism seems to take over.

If we apply this dialectic of determinism and voluntarism to the interpretation of Soviet history, two conclusions stand out very clearly: First, the early years—from 1917 until the late 20's when the country had irrevocably committed itself to forced industrialization and collectivization of agriculture—were a "voluntarist" period during which the Bolshevik Party and its leaders, meaning primarily Lenin and Stalin, played a decisive role in shaping the course of events. There were of course definite limits to what could have been done after the Bolsheviks came to power, but they were wide enough to encompass the course which was actually followed under Stalin at one extreme, and at the other extreme a course (certainly feasible and actually advocated by Bukharin and others in the Bolshevik leadership) of "socialist laissez faire" which would have involved surrender to the kulak-dominated market economy and most likely a relatively rapid restoration of capitalism.

The second conclusion which stands out is that in recent years—at least since the 20th Party Congress and the beginning of de-Stalinization—the Soviet Union has entered a "determinist" period in which the Party and its leaders are hardly more than cogs in a great machine which is running, sometimes smoothly and sometimes bumpily, along a more or less clearly prescribed course, some of the main aspects of which have been analyzed above.

Now it is clear that the kind of machine which came into being to dominate the "determinist" period was formed in the "voluntarist" period by the conscious decisions and acts of the Party leadership, for the most part after Stalin took over. This is not to imply that Stalin had a blueprint of the kind of society he wanted to create and shaped his policies accordingly, though considerations of this kind may have played some role. Between 1928 and the end of the Second World War, which was certainly the crucial formative period of present-day Soviet society, Stalin was probably mainly motivated by fear of external attack and a supposed need, in the face of this danger, to crush all actual or potential internal opposition. In other words, the kind of society being created in the Soviet Union during these years was in a real sense a by-product of policies designed to accomplish other ends. But, from our present point of view, this is not the important point. What is crucial is that these policies were deliberately decided upon and in no sense a mere reflex of an objective situation. They could have been different. The goal they were intended to achieve could have been different, and the combination of means designed to achieve the goal actually chosen or another goal or set of goals could also have been different. And the result today could have been a different society operating with a different internal logic and following a different course of development.

These are not mere armchair speculations. We *know* that different courses were possible in the decisive years after Lenin's death because we know that great struggles and debates racked the Bolshevik Party in that period. Nothing requires us to believe that Stalin's victory was inevitable, or that if the Left or Right Opposition had won out it would necessarily have followed the same course he followed. The options were real, and the Soviet Union is what it is today because some were embraced and others rejected.

This is not the occasion for a review of the arguments over what policies might have been adopted and their probable consequences: that would be an ambitious undertaking indeed. Suffice it to say that our own view is that Stalin was certainly right to make preparations to repel external aggression the number one priority, but that a different choice of means could have produced better results in the short run and much better results in the long run. More equality and fewer privileges to the bureaucracy, more trust and confidence in the masses, greater inner party democracy—these, we believe, could have been the guiding principles of a course which would have ensured the survival of the Soviet Union and pointed it toward, rather than away from, the luminous vision of a communist future.

Fifty years of Soviet history have many lessons to teach. And of these the greatest and most important, we believe, is that revolutionary societies can and must choose and that how they choose will unavoidably have fateful consequences for many years and decades to come.

44152